REVOLUTION AND SOCIALIST CONSTRUCTION IN KOREA

Selected Writings of

KIM IL SUNG

Selected Writings of
Kim Il Sung

Revolution and Socialist Construction in Korea

INTERNATIONAL PUBLISHERS
New York

Library of Congress Catalog Card Number: 75-152910
ISBN (cloth) 7178-0324-4; (paperback) 7178-0325-2
Printed in the United States of America

PUBLISHER'S NOTE

THE PRESENT selections have been made from the writings, speeches and reports of Premier Kim Il Sung during the period 1955 to 1970. In this brief span of 15 years the Democratic People's Republic of Korea, recovering from the war of 1950-53, went on to perform no less than a miracle—the transformation of a backward rural country into a modern industrial socialist state. By the end of the war, indiscriminate and unrestricted "saturation" bombing of the North by U.S. ground, air and naval power left intact hardly a city, village, factory or school, indeed any building of solid structure. It was a national calamity of unimaginable proportions.

Although democratic reforms and initial steps toward socialism had taken place in the five years between the end of World War II and the outbreak of the Korean War, the recovery from the latter opened the period of reconstruction of the economy and society which led to the emergence of a modern socialist society. The writings collected here, therefore, convey the theoretical thinking, policies and methods which are distinctive for this entire period of socialist formation in North Korea.

It may be helpful to the reader in following the text to outline the principal phases of this development, corresponding to the central objectives of each planning period. The Three-Year Plan, 1954-56, was devoted to recovery from the war and to the restoration of prewar levels of production. On overfulfillment of this plan, there followed the Five-Year Plan, 1957-61, to complete the first stage of industrialization and cooperative farming, laying the basis for a complete socialist economy. The Seven-Year Plan, 1962-68, had as its purpose to convert North Korea into a modern industrial socialist state, with an advanced agriculture, as the result of a deep-going technical revolution. Due to new dangers of war, it was decided at the Party Conference in 1966 to put off the completion of this plan for three years, to allow for extended and simultaneous defense construction. With both tasks—socialist construction and defense preparations "in parallel"—completed, Premier Kim Il Sung announced the new Six-Year Plan at the Fifth Party Congress in November 1970, which is described in the last chapter of this book. Corresponding to each of these phases of development, there were set forth new objectives in standards of living, in the cultural revolution, popular and specialized education, and in the ideological battle for socialist ideas.

These selections have also been chosen with an eye to presenting the major theoretical works of Kim Il Sung and what is unique and distinctive in his views on international matters and on questions of interest to all students of Marxism-Leninism and of comparative socialist societies.

The selections have been made from English texts published in Pyongyang, but they have been completely edited afresh. All footnotes are by the Editor. Common usages in Korean literature have been retained, e.g.—"Liberation" refers to the overthrow of Japanese colonial rule in 1945; "the war" or the "Fatherland Liberation War" to the Korean War of 1950-53; the "armistice" to the one negotiated at the end of that war.

CONTENTS

Prologue

TEN-POINT PROGRAM OF THE ASSOCIATION FOR RESTORATION OF THE FATHERLAND
(May 5, 1936)

1. A broad anti-Japanese united front shall be formed through the general mobilization of the Korean nation to overthrow the rule of predatory Japanese imperialism and to establish a genuine people's government of Korea.

2. Japan and its puppet "Manchukuo" shall be overthrown by the Koreans resident in Manchuria through a close alliance of the Korean and Chinese nations, and a genuine national autonomy shall be effected by the Koreans resident within Chinese territory.

3. The Japanese army, gendarmerie and police and their lackeys shall be disarmed and a revolutionary army which can fight truly for the independence of Korea shall be formed.

4. All the enterprises, railways, banks, ships, farms and irrigation facilities owned by the Japanese government and Japanese individuals, and all the properties and land of the traitorous

---

This Program was adopted at the formation of the Association in May 1936 which took place in an area of Manchuria bordering on Korea. It marked the beginning of the Anti-Japanese united front, corresponding to the anti-imperialist, anti-feudal, democratic stage of the revolution. In January 1937 the National Liberation Union was formed in Korea as a branch of the Association.

pro-Japanese elements shall be confiscated to obtain funds for the independence movement and, partly, for the relief of the poor.

5. All debts and taxes and the monopoly system imposed by the Japanese and their lackeys on the people shall be abolished, the living conditions of the masses improved, and national industry, agriculture and trade developed smoothly.

6. Freedom of speech, the press, assembly and association shall be won; pursuance of the terrorist policy and encouragement of feudalistic thoughts by the Japanese shall be rejected, and all political offenders released.

7. Inequality between the nobility and the commoners and other inequalities shall be removed, human equality irrespective of sex, nationality and religion assured; the social status of women shall be elevated and their personality respected.

8. Slave labor and slave education shall be abolished, forced military service and military education of the youth and children rejected, education carried on in our spoken and written language, and compulsory free education introduced.

9. The eight-hour day shall be introduced, working conditions improved, wages raised, a labor law adopted, a law on various kinds of insurance for the workers enacted by the state, and the unemployed working masses granted relief.

10. A close alliance shall be formed with those nations and states that approach the Korean nation on an equal footing, and comradely friendship maintained with those states and nations that express good will and neutrality toward our national liberation movement.

REVOLUTION AND SOCIALIST CONSTRUCTION IN KOREA

Selected Writings of
KIM IL SUNG

I.

CHARACTER AND TASKS OF OUR REVOLUTION

1. CHARACTER OF THE REVOLUTION AT THE PRESENT STAGE

AFTER THEIR liberation from the shackles of the protracted colonial rule of Japanese imperialism, the Korean people came to enjoy genuine freedom and opened a new historical phase of independence and prosperity for their country.

However, the U.S. Army, as soon as it landed in the southern half of our country, revived the Japanese imperialist ruling machine. It mobilized the landlords, comprador capitalists, pro-Japanese and pro-American elements, and traitors to the nation—hateful enemies of the Korean people—suppressed the people's committees formed on the initiative of the people soon after Liberation, as well as the patriotic democratic forces. The U.S. military followed a colonial policy, opposing the building of a unified, independent state by the Korean people. As a result, the Korean revolution has taken on a complex, arduous and protracted character.

In view of the situation obtaining in the country, our Party, taking advantage of the favorable conditions created by the great Soviet Army,* set out to build a powerful revolutionary demo-

---

*At the end of World War II, Soviet troops were stationed in the North and U.S. troops in the South, and a Joint Soviet-U.S. Committee was set up by agreement at the Moscow Conference of Foreign Ministers of the Soviet Union, the United States and Britain to facilitate the unification of Korea under a single democratic government. After the violation of the agreement by the United States with the

---

From *Every Effort for the Country's Unification and Independence and for Socialist Construction in the Northern Half of the Republic. Theses on the Character and Tasks of Our Revolution.* April 1955.

cratic base in the northern half of the Republic to serve as the foundation for the country's unification.

Fundamental to every revolution is the question of power. After Liberation, the working class in the northern half under the leadership of our Party formed a broad united front with all social sectors opposing imperialism and feudalism, and, on the basis of a solid alliance with the toiling peasants, set up the people's power.

The people's power, which was formed by the masses themselves, defined its basic tasks—to oppose foreign forces of aggression, to exercise dictatorship over the pro-Japanese and pro-American elements, the traitors to the nation, the landlords and comprador capitalists, the inveterate enemies of the Korean people, and steadily to consolidate the democratic system which assures freedom and happiness for the people, while rallying around itself all strata of patriotic democratic forces with the working class, the most advanced class, as its leading force. The people's power led the entire nation in the struggle for the fulfillment of these tasks.

Guided by our Party and supported by various social strata, the people's power liquidated the remnant forces of Japanese imperialism. It carried out the historic land reform, confiscating the land of the landlord class that had helped the imperialists impose their influence, and distributed it among the broad sections of the peasantry without payment. It confiscated industries, railway transport, communications, banks, etc., formerly owned by the Japanese imperialists, pro-Japanese elements and traitors to the nation, and turned them into the property of the entire people. It enacted the Labor Law, the Law on the Equality of the Sexes, the Law on Agricultural Tax in Kind, and other social legislation; effected the democratization of judicial organs and educational institutions; promoted the development of a progressive national culture and art; and founded the people's armed forces.

separate elections in the South in 1948, the Democratic People's Republic of Korea was established on September 8, 1948, and Soviet troops withdrew in December of the same year. (*See* Wilfred G. Burchett, *Again Korea*, New York, 1968.)

As a result, the tasks of the anti-imperialist and anti-feudal democratic revolution were fulfilled in the northern half, where the people gradually entered the period of transition to socialism.

But the struggle of the people in the North for the gradual transition to socialism was obstructed by the three-year war unleashed by the U.S. imperialists and the Syngman Rhee clique,* and, thus, the transition required a long period of time.

The war was a crucial and harsh trial for the democratic system our people had established and for the people themselves.

The victory of the democratic revolution in the northern half and the achievements of its people in economic construction constituted the great force that made it possible to repulse the armed invasion of the U.S. imperialists and their lackey, the traitorous Syngman Rhee clique, and to safeguard the democratic base in the North, the fountainhead of the revolution in our country.

To this day, however, when we are celebrating the 10th Anniversary of the Liberation, our country has not yet been unified, the territory and nation remain divided in two and the southern half has been turned into a colony of the U.S. imperialists.

The imperialist aggressors still remain in South Korea and, implacably set against the peaceful unification of our country, constantly create tension in Korea, reinforcing Syngman Rhee's puppet army under the slogan, "March North and Unify."

Under the ROK-U.S. Agreement on Military and Economic Assistance, concluded recently by the United States and the traitorous Syngman Rhee clique, the imperialists are pursuing the policy of colonial plunder more openly.

The traitorous Syngman Rhee gang is selling the "custodian properties"** to foreign capitalists, compradors and profiteers,

---

*Syngman Rhee, a protege of the United States, was made the head of state as the result of a separate election in South Korea which was held under UN supervision.

**The "custodian properties" consist of the assets formerly held by the Japanese in Korea and confiscated by the U.S. Military Government in 1945, but later turned over to the Syngman Rhee regime when it was formed in 1948. These properties were estimated to account for 80 percent of the total assets in South Korea in 1945.

and guarantees free investment of foreign capital in South Korea under its "Constitution."

In the southern half today, industry is almost at a standstill, and the workers are suffering from appalling slave labor and unemployment. The countryside has been devastated and exploitation by the landlords is intensified. Prices are skyrocketing, and the people, denied even the faintest semblance of freedom, are distressed by hunger and poverty.

The situation prevailing in the South, along with the territorial division of the country and the splitting of the nation, brings to the entire people of South Korea immeasurable miseries and suffering and hinders the normal social development of a united country.

Hence, the basic tasks of our revolution at the present stage are to overthrow the aggressive forces of U.S. imperialism and their lackeys and allies—the landlords, comprador capitalists, pro-Japanese and pro-American elements, and traitors to the nation—in the southern half, and to free the people there from imperialist and feudal oppression and exploitation, thereby achieving the country's unification along democratic lines and attaining complete national independence.

In the South, the motive forces of the revolution consist of the working class and its most reliable ally, the peasantry, and the broad sections of the small propertied classes opposed to U.S. imperialism and the feudal forces. And even a considerable number of national capitalists can join in the anti-imperialist, anti-feudal struggle.

The enemies of the revolution are the aggressive forces of U.S. imperialism, and the landlords, comprador capitalists, pro-Japanese and pro-American elements, and traitors to the nation in the South who abet, and are allied with, those forces.

Were it not for interference by the United States, the chieftain of world reaction, the Korean people would long ago have overthrown the domestic reactionary forces and triumphantly fulfilled the tasks of the anti-imperialist and anti-feudal democratic revolution throughout Korea.

We cannot fulfil the tasks of the revolution without driving the U.S. imperialists out of our country, and without liquidating their running dogs, the Syngman Rhee clique.

Our revolution, therefore, has to carry out the task of anti-imperialist national liberation on the one hand and, on the other, the anti-feudal task of liberating the broad sections of the peasantry in the southern half who are still oppressed and exploited by the landlords.

In the conditions prevailing in the South today, particularly under circumstances in which it has been turned into a U.S. imperialist colony, our revolution will be carried out through a nationwide struggle of an arduous, protracted nature.

We have to rally all the revolutionary forces and launch a strenuous struggle to drive out the aggressive forces of U.S. imperialism, crush the traitorous Syngman Rhee gang which is under its thumb, and win victory in the revolution.

Today, the might of the camp of peace, democracy and socialism headed by the Soviet Union is growing every day. Its internationalist solidarity is strengthened and has become invincible, whereas the imperialist camp is becoming ever weaker owing to its internal contradictions and mutual conflicts. The outcome depends on how well we strengthen, organize and mobilize our forces under the banner of internationalism and hasten the downfall of imperialism.

We must strengthen still more our Party, people's power and public organizations, unite more firmly around our Party all the patriotic, democratic forces of the people in the North and the South and rouse them to a nationwide revolutionary struggle against the U.S. imperialists and the Syngman Rhee gang. We must further consolidate the democratic base in the North, the fountainhead of our revolution, politically, economically and militarily, and turn it not only into a force powerful enough to defend the northern half of the Republic against aggression by imperialism and its running dogs but also into a decisive force for attaining the unification and independence of our country. For this purpose, we must further advance the revolution and carry out thoroughly the tasks of building the foundations of socialism in the North.

Gradual transition to socialism is an inevitable demand of the social and economic development in the North.

To strengthen the democratic base, it is necessary to increase the productive forces of industry and agriculture rapidly and further raise the material and cultural standards of the people. The small commodity and capitalist economies that still remain in our country hinder the growth of the productive forces. In particular, the private peasant economy predominant in the countryside constitutes a big obstacle to the speedy rehabilitation and future development of agriculture. Without transforming the peasant economy and private trade and industry along socialist lines, it is impossible to ensure the development of the productive forces, radically improve the people's livelihood and further cement the unity and solidarity of all the people based on the worker-peasant alliance led by the working class.

The state and cooperative economies, which are predominant in the national economy in the northern half, exert a decisive influence upon the small commodity economy based on private ownership and the capitalist economy which makes up a small proportion of the total, leading them inevitably to the road of socialist transformation.

Thus, the social and economic conditions in the North at the present stage raise the building of socialism as an inevitable demand of social development.

Socialist construction in the northern half will be a great inspiration to the people in the South, especially to the workers, peasants and broad sections of the small propertied classes, and conducive to the formation of a united front even with some of the national capitalists in the South.

The successes gained in socialist construction in the northern half will not only be a decisive force in achieving the unification of the country, but also a strong material guarantee for speedily rehabilitating and developing the economy in the southern half and ensuring socialist construction on a nationwide scale after the country is unified

2. TASKS OF CONSOLIDATING THE REVOLUTIONARY DEMOCRATIC BASE AND BUILDING SOCIALISM

Economic Forms and Class Relations in the North

Socio-economic conditions in the northern half underwent a radical change as a result of the democratic reforms effected after Liberation. At the present stage, the socio-economic forms in the northern half can be classified into three main categories: (1) the socialist economic form; (2) the small commodity economic form; (3) the capitalist economic form.

The socialist economic form is composed of state and cooperative economies. Today, the socialist economic form constitutes the leading force in the northern half and it holds a predominant position in industry in particular. At present, the state economy represents some 90 per cent of total industrial production in our country and the cooperative economy 7-8 per cent.

Human relations in the socialist economic form are characterized by comradely cooperation and assistance among the working people who are freed from exploitation. They do not work for the enrichment of the exploiters as in the past, but engage in free, honorable labor for themselves, for the prosperity and progress of their country, and get their share according to the quality and quantity of labor expended. Here the economic laws of socialism operate and production grows according to plan, serving the ever-increasing material and cultural needs of the working people.

The small commodity economic form is composed of the individual peasant economy which still predominates in agriculture, and of the urban handicraft economy. At the present stage of the transition period, the majority of the population of our country is embraced in the small commodity economic form.

Small commodity production is based on private ownership of the means of production and individual labor. The petty bourgeoisie can be remolded along socialist lines although they vacillate between the two paths, socialism and capitalism, because of their dual nature. Especially in our country the petty bourgeoisie received benefits directly from the land reform and other democratic reforms, and are remolding themselves voluntarily into socialist working people (either workers or cooperative members) with the rapid growth of the socialist economic form in the national economy, realizing by experience the superiority of the people's democratic system and the correctness of our Party and Government policies.

The capitalist economic form is composed of individually-owned capitalist trade and industry in the towns and the rich-farmer economy in the countryside. It is the form of exploitation still remaining in the northern half of the Republic. In this economic form the economic laws of capitalism operate within a limited range.

In the national economy of the northern half, the capitalist economic form constitutes an extremely small proportion compared with the socialist economic form. Particularly in the field of industry all private ownership accounts for no more than 2-3 per cent of industrial production, and even this consists mostly of small-scale enterprises limited to such secondary branches as rice refining, cotton ginning, etc. As the socialist economic form grows and develops in the national economy in the northern half, the capitalist economic form is being gradually transformed along socialist lines.

Because the small commodity economic form still remains in the rural districts at present, class differentiation of the peasantry is taking place more or less, and rich farmers are emerging and increasing. They employ hired labor either seasonally or permanently, and exploit the poor peasants by manipulating the grain market, by covertly lending money and various goods at usurious rates, and exacting heavy charges for the use of farm implements and draught animals, etc.

But the economic foothold of the rich farmers is extremely weak, for the land reform was carried out under the slogan, "Land to the tillers!" Particularly, with cooperatives growing rapidly in the rural areas, objects of exploitation by the rich farmers are disappearing. These circumstances will bring them to join the agricultural cooperatives voluntarily and to be remolded gradually into toiling peasants. Yet this will not be realized smoothly without class struggle in the countryside; it will entail the struggle against certain resistance on the part of the enemy.

Such are the fundamental features of the economic structure of a transitional character and the objective laws of social and economic development in the northern half of the Republic. This determines the policy of our Party for socialist construction.

Tasks of Our Party in Laying the Foundations of Socialism in the Northern Half

The basic task confronting our Party at the present stage of the period of transition to socialism is to lay the foundations of socialism on the basis of the achievements gained in the struggle for the postwar rehabilitation and development of the national economy, while further consolidating the worker-peasant alliance.

We should expand and strengthen the predominant position of the socialist economic form in all spheres of the national economy by gradually transforming the small commodity and capitalist economic forms along socialist lines, and should further develop the productive forces to lay the material and technical foundations of socialism.

To this end, it is necessary to eliminate the colonial one-sidedness and technical backwardness of industry and build up the foundation for socialist industrialization. The building of the foundation of socialist industrialization signifies the completion of the first stage of industrialization in our country.

The keynote of socialist industrialization lies in the priority development of heavy industry. Only with the establishment of a powerful heavy industry is it possible to ensure the development of all industries, transport and agriculture, and the victory of the socialist system.

The backwardness and deformation of our heavy industry, the legacy of Japanese imperialist colonial rule, hampered the development of the economy as a whole in our country after Liberation and severely obstructed a proportionate development of heavy industry, light industry and agriculture in particular.

If we do not set up a powerful heavy industry in our country in the future, we shall not be able to shore up light industry which was originally very backward, nor provide the countryside with modern farm machinery, nor ensure radical improvement in the people's living conditions. Only with the establishment of a powerful heavy industry, can the independence of the economy and the independent progress of the country be assured.

In the rural economy, the individual peasant economy should be converted into a socialist collective economy by gradually enlisting the peasants in agricultural cooperatives on the voluntary principle. Unless the rural economy is developed along the line of socialist collectivization, agriculture cannot catch up with the fast developing industry, cannot supply it with raw materials and labor reserves, and so will hamper industrial development in the long run, and, accordingly, will obstruct the overall socio-economic development in the northern half. At the same time, unless the rural economy is transformed into a socialist collective economy, it will be impossible to improve rapidly the living standard of the peasants, eliminate rich farmers and other exploiting elements that are reviving in the countryside, and consolidate our Party's rural positions.

Handicrafts and small private trade should be transformed gradually along socialist lines through the cooperative economy.

The capitalist elements still remaining in town and country will have to be restricted and utilized, and remolded, step by step, along socialist lines.

And not only should the production bond between industry and agriculture be strengthened, but their economic ties should also be expanded and strengthened through the market.

Along with this, the masses of the people should be educated in socialist ideology, and new technical and cultural workers trained in large numbers from among them.

In order to carry out these tasks after the war, our Party marked off three main stages in the rehabilitation and construction of the war-ravaged national economy and has been waging a struggle for carrying out those tasks successfully.

For postwar rehabilitation and development of the national economy, our Party set the following stages: the preparatory stage of six months to one year for overall restoration and construction; the stage for carrying out a Three-Year Plan designed to rehabilitate completely all branches of the national economy from war damage and attain the prewar level of industrial and agricultural production; and the stage for the implementation of a Five-Year Plan which will lay the foundation for socialist industrialization.

Our Party set down as the basic line of postwar economic construction to assure the priority growth of heavy industry with simultaneous development of light industry and agriculture.

During the Three-Year Plan, we are following in the field of industry the policy of concentrating our efforts on those branches of heavy industry closely associated with the improvement of the people's livelihood, laying emphasis on the restoration of destroyed factories and mills and, at the same time, rebuilding them on the basis of new technique and constructing some new ones. It was decided that the destroyed factories should not be restored mechanically on original sites; some factories should be restored in their former locales for the sake of speedy rehabilitation and economy, but factories and mills to be built anew should be distributed with consideration for their organic connection with our country's sources of raw materials, transportation facilities and existing industrial establishments.

In 1956, the last year of the Three-Year Plan, the total value of industrial output is scheduled at 1.5 times over the prewar year of 1949, with the output of the means of production increasing 1.3 times and consumer goods by two times. To assure this growth of industrial production, funds amounting to 37,360 million *won** are to be invested in the field of industry in the three years.

During the Three-Year Plan, not only will the old factories and

---

*A North Korean *won* is valued at U.S. 40 cents.

enterprises be restored, but also many new machine factories will be built and light industry will also be rehabilitated and developed speedily.

By 1956, a new textile mill equipped with 60 to 100 thousand spindles with an annual production capacity of 40 to 80 million meters of fabric, as well as canneries, meat-packing factories and many other light industry plants will be built.

The Three-Year National Economic Plan envisages enormous state support for the rapid rehabilitation and development of the rural economy and its socialist transformation. During the Three-Year Plan, 5,575 million *won* will be invested in the rural economy, of which 2,225 million *won* will go into irrigation projects.

The speedy development of agriculture will supply the population with more food and provide more raw materials to light industry. In 1956, total grain output will surpass the level of the prewar year 1949 by 19 per cent, of which total rice output will increase by 30 per cent.

The rapid rehabilitation and development of industry and agriculture during the Three-Year Plan will meet the population's increasing needs for the necessities of life and create the necessary conditions for abolishing the rationing of food and industrial goods and for switching over to free trade.

In the sphere of education and culture, conditions will be created for the introduction of the system of universal, compulsory primary education and the number of university and college students will reach 22,500 in the period of the Three-Year Plan. National culture and the arts will be developed further; theaters, cinema houses and clubs with a total seating capacity of 134,000 will be restored or newly built.

By 1956, the last year of the Three-Year Plan, the national economy which was destroyed by the war will be rehabilitated in the main and, thus, in the northern half the postwar rehabilitation period will come to an end. Industry and agriculture restored in this period will become the solid base for refashioning completely our country's economy into the socialist economy in the future.

The central task of the First Five-Year Plan for Development of the National Economy, which will be worked out on this basis later, is to build the foundations of socialism in our country.

In the field of heavy industry, the iron works not yet fully restored in the Three-Year Plan period will, first of all, be completely rehabilitated during the Five-Year Plan so as to produce approximately 1,000,000 tons of pig iron annually, and the machine-building industry will be developed to produce 2,000 machine tools annually.

It is envisaged that in 1961, the last year of the Five-Year Plan, the total generating capacity will be 1,850,000 kw. and the output of coal 8.5-9 million tons.

Our chemical industry will supply the state with more than 400,000 tons of fertilizer.

In the period of the Five-Year Plan, the underground resources of our country will be tapped for larger quantities of raw materials to help build the foundations of socialism, and they will become the main source of foreign currency.

During the Five-Year Plan the necessities of life will be turned out in larger quantities for the improvement of the people's welfare.

In the field of light industry, chief attention will be paid in the Five-Year Plan period to the production of textiles and processed foodstuffs which are the main necessities of life. In 1961, the output of different kinds of fabric will be 150 million meters, or about 15 meters per head of the population in the northern half of the Republic, and vegetable and meat processing factories and flour mills will be built in the vicinity of major cities.

In the field of agriculture, 3.5 million tons of grain, 150,000 tons of meat, 150,000 tons of sugar beet, 50,000 tons of cotton, 80,000 tons of fruit and 30,000 tons of cocoons will be produced during the Five-Year Plan. Thus the question of food will be solved in the northern half and the requirements of light industry for raw materials will be more fully satisfied.

During the Five-Year Plan, agriculture will be cooperativized as a whole in the northern half of the Republic, thereby eliminating the roots of exploitation and poverty in the countryside and completing the socialist transformation of the rural economy.

For the carrying out of this tremendous plan, we need many cadres who are politically seasoned and possess advanced science and techniques. In 1961, the last year of the Five-Year Plan, we must have over 130,000 highly qualified engineers and assistant engineers.

To lay the foundations of socialism in the northern half is a huge and difficult job. But led by the Workers Party of Korea, the Korean people will be able to carry out this great task successfully.

Under the leadership of our Party, the political and moral unity of the broad masses of the people, on the basis of the worker-peasant alliance, with the working class as its core, is taking shape and developing, and socialist construction in the northern half enjoys the active support of the millions of working people.

We have precious experience—accumulated during the five years of prewar peaceful construction and in the struggle for the postwar rehabilitation and construction of the national economy—and one million Party members and the heroic people who were tried and seasoned in the harsh three-year war.

Our country also abounds in natural resources necessary for socialist construction.

Not only can we draw on the advanced experience of the Soviet Union, the People's Republic of China and the People's Democracies, but we also receive great economic and technical assistance from them.

All these are favorable subjective and objective conditions for socialist construction in the northern half of our country.

But there are obstacles and difficulties in our socialist construction, too.

Industry in our country has a very short history, and it was completely destroyed in the war. The abundant resources have not yet been developed fully and there is an acute shortage of cadres in industry.

The cultural standard of our people is still low, and the

survivals of outdated thoughts have not been obliterated from the minds of men.

Our socialist construction is proceeding under conditions in which the northern half, an industrial zone, is artifically separated from the southern half, an agricultural zone, and U.S. imperialism, the chieftain of international reaction, still occupies the southern half, making frantic efforts to disrupt construction in the North.

Surmounting all these obstacles and difficulties, we should and can successfully carry out the task of building the foundations of socialism.

The Workers Party of Korea is the organizer and inspirer of all the victories of the Korean people. The organizational and ideological consolidation of our Party is the guarantee of our victory in the struggle for the unification and independence of the country and for socialist construction in the northern half of the Republic.

Further to consolidate the Party organizationally and ideologically, it is imperative to assure steel-strong unity and solidarity of the Party ranks, strengthen Party discipline and further to promote inner-Party democracy. The promotion of inner-Party democracy can be assured only if the work of the Party committees is improved and the collective leadership of the Party strengthened. All Party members and leading cadres should observe the principle of collective Party leadership, and wage a resolute struggle against any and every tendency toward individualist heroics and liberalism which runs counter to it.

All Party members should arm themselves more firmly with Marxist-Leninist theory, systematically study the history of our Party and its decisions, and earnestly study and assimilate the experience gained in the building of socialism by the Communist Party of the Soviet Union and other communist and workers parties of the fraternal countries, tirelessly learn theories on economic construction, acquire knowledge of science and technology, and elevate their practical abilities and cultural standards.

To carry the Party's line and policies into effect, we have to strengthen further our state power based on the worker-peasant alliance under working-class leadership.

The U.S. imperialists occupying the southern half of the Republic and their minions, the domestic reactionary forces, are trying to use every conceivable means to oppose the unification and independence of the country and undermine the building of the foundations of socialism in the northern half.

Only by strengthening the organs of state power is it possible to rally the masses of the people around the Party and the Government more firmly, suppress the resistance of the enemies of the revolution thoroughly, and carry out the cause of socialist construction more successfully. The strengthening of the dictatorship over counter-revolutionaries, spies, wreckers and saboteurs and the promotion of democracy among the masses of the people are important conditions for the successful carrying out of socialist construction.

One of the most important tasks our Party must fulfil is to strengthen further our people's armed forces.

Only by strengthening our People's Army, is it possible for us to defend firmly the precious achievements the people have won by their sweat and blood and our democratic base from the enemy's encroachment, and to ensure the successful carrying out of socialist construction. Therefore, our Party should do everything in its power to train the People's Army into a steel-strong cadre army and intensify the support of the entire people for it.

Our Party's line and policies for the country's unification and independence, and for socialist construction in the northern half of the Republic, illuminate the path for the entire Korean people to follow.

Under the leadership of our Party, the Korean people have always won victories in their arduous struggle, surmounting all difficulties and trials. No force on earth can prevent our people, united solidly around the Party, from marching forward to a bright future along the path indicated by the Party.

The Korean people, led by our Party and holding aloft the

banner of Marxism-Leninism and proletarian internationalism, will surely be victorious in their just struggle for the unification and independence of the country and for socialism by strengthening their solidarity with the peoples of the camp of peace, democracy and socialism headed by the Soviet Union, and by augmenting further their own revolutionary forces.

II

COMPLETION OF
SOCIALIST TRANSFORMATION

AGRICULTURAL COOPERATIVES, HANDICRAFTS AND TRADE

THE SOCIALIST transformation of the old economy is a law-governed process in the development of the socialist revolution, a cardinal task that has to be accomplished in the period of transition from capitalism to socialism.

With the successful carrying out of the anti-imperialist, anti-feudal democratic revolution in the northern part of the country after the Liberation, North Korea gradually embarked on the path of transition to socialism; socialist transformation began at that time.

Before the war, however, because the necessary social, economic and material conditions were not yet fully matured, socialist transformation was only partial, the main work being to prepare for it. In the postwar years socialist transformation of agriculture, handicrafts, capitalist trade and industry was undertaken on a full scale and in 1958 it was completed in all these fields almost simultaneously.

Most important in socialist transformation is the cooperative reorganization of agriculture, all the more so in our country where the peasantry made up the majority of the population.

In the immediate post-armistice days private farming predominated, the socialist sector constituting a small proportion. So long as small commodity production dominates in the countryside, the source of exploitation and poverty cannot be removed, nor can

From *Report on the Work of the Central Committee to the Fourth Congress of the Workers Party of Korea.* September 11, 1961.

the life of the peasantry radically be improved. It is impossible for small and scattered private farming to develop in a planned way and employ advanced technique extensively, and in most cases expanded reproduction is impossible.

All the limitations of our private farming were manifest most strikingly in the postwar years, and they could not be allowed to exist any longer. Owing to the war, the material foundations of agriculture were seriously undermined, farming was fragmented further and a shortage of labor and draught animals was keenly felt. Under these circumstances, further maintenance of private farming would make it impossible to restore rapidly the ruined productive forces of agriculture and, above all, to solve the food problem. There was the danger that the contradictions between socialist state industry and private farming would give rise to a disparity between industry, which was being rapidly rehabilitated and developed in the postwar period, and agriculture which was being rehabilitated very slowly. Besides, on the basis of small farming it was impossible rapidly to improve the life of the impoverished peasantry, and all the more was it impossible to solve the problem of the poor peasants whose number had increased during the war.

The only way to release the agricultural productive forces completely from the shackles of the old relations of production and to free the peasants from exploitation and poverty once and for all lies in the socialist cooperation of agriculture. The postwar situation in our country demanded that this be done without delay. The peasants themselves came to realize, through their own hardships, that they could not live in the old way any longer. That is why our Party put forward the task of agricultural cooperation immediately after the armistice, and energetically pushed it forward on the strength of the increasing enthusiasm of the peasantry.

Most important in leading the agricultural cooperative movement are strict adherence to the Leninist voluntary principle and the promotion of the movement by proving to the peasants by practical example the advantages of cooperative farming.

In the immediate post-armistice days the poor peasants were

the most active supporters of agricultural cooperation. In a tentative way, our Party first organized and consolidated a few agricultural cooperatives in each county by relying on the poor peasants and core Party members in the countryside. In the course of this work we were able to determine correctly the specific methods and tempo of cooperation suitable to the actual conditions of our country. At the same time our cadres accumulated experience and became confident in leading the cooperative movement. Besides, we could persuade the masses of the peasantry, particularly the middle peasants, and lead them to join the cooperatives of their own free will by demonstrating in practice the advantages of cooperative farming on the basis of their own experience.

In agricultural cooperation the voluntary principle was followed not only with the middle peasants but with all sections of the rural population, the rich peasants included. Taking into consideration the specific conditions of our villages, where the rich peasant economy was very weak, our Party took the line of gradually remolding rich peasants in keeping with the developing cooperative movement, while restricting their exploiting practices. We admitted into the cooperative farms all the rich peasants who accepted socialist transformation and were willing to work honestly. We took appropriate measures against the handful who sought to hinder the movement. At the last stage of the movement, when the cooperatives had gained in scope and strength and there was no longer any one to exploit in the villages, the majority of rich peasants joined the cooperatives voluntarily.

Thus, in drawing various sections of the peasantry into cooperative farming on the basis of object lessons and the voluntary principle, our Party consistently adhered to the correct class policy of firmly relying on the poor peasants, strengthening the alliance with the middle peasants, and restricting and gradually remolding the rich peasants. We saw to it that poor peasants served as the nucleus in all agricultural cooperatives, and took care to avoid the organization of cooperatives exclusively with relatively well-to-do peasants or situations in which the work of cooperative management came under the influence of the rich peasants. On the other hand, we took strict precautions against the tendency to weaken our alliance with the middle peasants by forcing them into cooperatives or encroaching upon their interests.

Such measures prevented possible losses that might be caused by deep-going changes in the countryside, developed the cooperative movement on a sound basis, and assured a steady growth in agricultural production.

Adherence to the voluntary principle in the agricultural cooperative movement does not mean in any sense that the movement should be left to the mercy of spontaneity. As is the case with the socialist system in general, the cooperative system in the countryside will not come of itself nor will it be strengthened and developed spontaneously. What is needed here is strong leadership and assistance by the Party and the state.

In order to promote the agricultural cooperative movement, our Party persistently carried out organizational and political work among the peasantry and exerted tremendous efforts to reinforce the newly established cooperative economy politically and economically.

We strengthened the Party organizations in the villages, trained and assigned a large number of management personnel to the cooperatives. We gave effective leadership to the establishment of a socialist system and order in the cooperatives and to the advancement of the socialist consciousness of their members.

Lenin said that every social system arises only with the financial assistance of a definite class; the social system which the socialist state must now assist more than usual is the cooperative system. In keeping with Lenin's teaching, we gave all-out state assistance to the agricultural cooperatives. The powerful material assistance given by the state to the peasantry on the basis of the rapid development of socialist industry played a decisive role in giving support to the weak agricultural cooperatives which had been organized only with poor peasants at an early stage, in proving their superiority over private farming, and in economically reinforcing the cooperatives whose number grew rapidly in a brief period.

Only by relying on the firm leadership of the Party and the working class and on the powerful support from socialist state-run industry was it possible to overcome the innumerable difficulties in the postwar years, lead millions of peasants onto the path of socialist collectivization, and assure a firm victory for the socialist system of cooperative economy in our countryside.

Even after the completion of the cooperative transformation of agriculture, the system of cooperative economy should continue to advance, making constant progress and striving for perfection.

Our agricultural cooperatives were organized on a relatively small scale. Our Party saw to it that a cooperative was organized with no more than 40 to 100 peasant households. The Party did not allow cooperatives to be organized or amalgamated on too big a scale. This was in full accord with conditions at a time when our farming technique was still backward, and the qualifications of the management personnel were still inadequate, their experience insufficient.

But the comparatively small cooperatives gradually became incompatible with the further growth of the productive forces of agriculture, and particularly with its requirements of technical reconstruction. There arose the necessity of enlarging the size of agricultural cooperatives by appropriate amalgamations. As they were strengthened politically and economically and the level of their management personnel was raised, amalgamation became an urgent demand, and the peasants themselves realized its necessity.

Hence, toward the end of 1958 the merger of cooperatives was carried out on the principle of one for each *ri**, with the chairman of the *ri* people's committee concurrently holding the chairmanship of the management board of the cooperative.

The enlargement of the agricultural cooperatives made it possible to use land and other means of production more effectively, introduce modern farm machines and advanced farming methods extensively, vigorously carry out nature-remaking pro-

*Smallest administrative unit.

jects for irrigation, afforestation and water conservation, improve organization of labor, and develop the cooperative economy in an all-round manner.

With the agricultural production unit becoming one with the administrative unit of *ri* and the *ri* people's committee chairman assuming concurrently the chairmanship of the cooperative, the *ri* people's committee concentrated its efforts on the consolidation of the agricultural cooperatives and the development of agricultural production. Accordingly, the role and functions of the local people's committees in building up the economy and culture generally were enhanced.

Along with the amalgamation of the agricultural cooperatives, the work of consumers' cooperatives and credit cooperatives was handed over to them. This enabled the agricultural cooperatives to plan and manage not only production but also commodity circulation and credit in an integrated way. Thus they were able to show greater independence and initiative in the development of the cooperative economy and the promotion of the well-being of cooperative members. In particular, with the agricultural cooperatives directly handling rural commerce, commodities were exchanged more smoothly between town and country, and the economic ties between industry and agriculture were consolidated.

Our agricultural cooperatives thus became a more advanced, solid socialist economy. From all the facts and experience, we can now say with confidence that, with regard to its organizational form and size, the cooperative economy established in our countryside is the most rational and advantageous socialist economy for the specific conditions of our country in the present period.

In order to bring about the complete sway of socialist production relations, we not only had to cooperativize private farming in the countryside but also carry out the socialist transformation of handicrafts and capitalist trade and industry in the towns.

In our country the socialist transformation of handicrafts was already undertaken on an experimental basis before the war.

After the Liberation, thanks to the assistance of the people's power, our handicraftsmen, bankrupt and ruined in the years of Japanese imperialist rule, restored and developed their economy and significantly improved their living conditions. Nevertheless, their economy, fragmented and technically backward, was not stable and had no prospects of development. The cooperative transformation of the scattered handicraft economy was the only way further to develop its production and technique and improve the living conditions of the handicraftsmen.

In 1947, in the early days of the transition period, our Party laid down the line of forming producers' cooperatives of handicraftsmen to reorganize their private economy into a socialist, cooperative economy. Thus, already before the war, initial successes had been registered and a certain amount of experience had been accumulated in the socialist transformation of the handicrafts.

Because most of the large state-run industrial establishments were destroyed during the [Korean] war, our Party devoted great attention to the expansion and development of cooperative industry alongside state-owned local industry in order to assure a stabilized life for the people. After the war the Party pushed forward more vigorously the movement for transforming the handicrafts on cooperative lines. The war had played havoc with the handicrafts, causing their further fragmentation. Unless they united their economy and relied on the active support of the state, the handicraftsmen could not improve their living conditions. Under these circumstances they actively supported our Party's line of cooperative transformation, the handicraft cooperative movement progressed rapidly, and was brought to a successful conclusion within a few years after the war.

The socialist reorganization of capitalist trade and industry, too, progressed rather smoothly in North Korea.

The prolonged colonial rule of the Japanese imperialists had hampered seriously the growth of national capital in our country. Japanese imperialist capital monopolized the major branches of our national economy; the economy of our national capitalists— except for a handful of comprador capitalists—was negligible.

After Liberation, as a result of the nationalization of industries, transport services, communications, banks, and so forth, which had belonged to the Japanese imperialists and the comprador capitalists, the socialist state sector became predominant in the national economy, and capitalist trade and industry were very weak from the beginning of the transition period. These circumstances provided us with favorable conditions for enlisting capitalist traders and industrialists in socialist construction and reorganizing their economy by peaceful means.

In the period of transition, our Party's policy in relation to capitalist trade and industry was to reorganize them gradually along socialist lines, turning to account their positive aspects, while restricting their negative ones.

In the period after the Korean War the problem of socialist transformation of capitalist trade and industry matured. Because of serious damage caused by the war, a considerable number of entrepreneurs and traders were ruined, and became factory or office workers in state-owned enterprises, while the remaining ones were reduced mostly to the status of handicraftsmen or petty merchants. Under these circumstances, the capitalist traders and industrialists found it impossible to restore their ruined enterprises unless they relied on the assistance of the state and the socialist economy, and unless they pooled their means of production, funds and efforts. Moreover, as agriculture and handicrafts were being transformed along cooperative lines, they could no longer obtain raw and other materials on the private market. Under conditions in which the socialist economic sector dominated all spheres of the national economy, it was impossible for a small number of private entrepreneurs and traders to maintain their private economy.

Only when they were included in the socialist system of the economy could the entrepreneurs and traders improve their condition, find a road to the future, and serve the state and society better.

Taking into consideration the specific conditions prevailing in North Korea, our Party mapped out the line of transforming capitalist trade and industry through different forms of cooperative economy. Realizing that this conformed with their interests and represented the correct path for them, the entrepreneurs and traders supported the Party's line of cooperation. Thus, the socialist reorganization of capitalist trade and industry was brought to completion in a short time.

Thanks to the Party's correct leadership and the active assistance of the state, the socialist reorganization of handicrafts and capitalist trade and industry was carried out successfully. By adhering strictly to the voluntary principle, the Party drew handicraftsmen and middle and small industrialists into various producers' cooperatives according to their respective trades. On the basis of preferential consolidation of the handicraftsmen's producers' cooperatives, entrepreneurs were gradually taken into the cooperative economy and here, in particular, the semi-socialist form was used broadly. In order to transform traders along socialist lines, marketing cooperatives or production-and-marketing cooperatives were formed and they were later reorganized into producers' cooperatives by increasing gradually the proportion of production.

In transforming private trade and industry along socialist lines, the Party closely combined the economic transformation with the remolding of individuals. Joining the producers' cooperatives, the entrepreneurs and traders broke completely with their former life in which they exploited others, and have been transformed into socialist working people who produce material wealth by their own labor. In this process, their ideological remolding also has been facilitated.

While carrying out vigorously the socialist transformation of handicrafts and capitalist trade and industry, we rendered tremendous state assistance in the consolidation of the producers' cooperatives thus organized. Thanks to the advantages of the socialist cooperative economy, the active help by the state and the devoted labor of their members, the economic foundations of the producers' cooperatives speedily have been reinforced, and their members' living standard improved further. Today, an important part is played by cooperative industry in the development of the national economy. Members of our producers' cooperatives are taking part in socialist construction with great pride and a high degree of enthusiasm as honored socialist working people.

With the completion of the socialist reorganization of agriculture, handicrafts and capitalist trade and industry, the socialist relations of production have established their complete sway in town and country. The productive forces have been freed entirely from the chains of the old relations of production, and exploitation of man by man has been liquidated for good.

We have established in the northern part of Korea a social system free from exploitation and oppression, the very system to which our working people had long aspired and for which many Korean Communists fought at the cost of their blood. This represents our people's greatest victory under the leadership of our Party.

An important feature of the socialist transformation in our country is that it was completed in so short a time, in only four or five years after the war, despite the relatively low level of the productive forces and technical backwardness.

Some dogmatists were once doubtful of our Party's policy of socialist transformation, and wavered. They held that "transformation of the relations of production is impossible without socialist industrialization," that "there can be no agricultural cooperation without up-to-date farm machinery," or that "the tempo of socialist transformation is too fast." They did not understand that the rapid progress of socialist transformation was a law-governed phenomenon which reflected the specific conditions of our country in the postwar period.

The socialist state economy developed rapidly on the basis of the land reform, nationalization of industries and other democratic reforms carried out after Liberation, and overwhelmingly dominated in industry and trade. The railways, communications, banking and foreign trade establishments were placed under state control from the first days of the transition period. The socialist sector, which held a dominant position in the national economy, exercised a decisive influence on the small commodity and capitalist economies, and led them onto the inevitable path of socialism. Particularly, the rapid development of state-run industry provided a material base capable of giving powerful support to the socialist reorganization of agriculture, handicrafts and capitalist trade and industry.

The balance of forces between the classes in the country also turned decisively in favor of socialism. In the postwar years the forces opposing socialist transformation in town and country were negligible. Our peasant masses were awakened politically and united firmly around the Party by the prolonged revolutionary struggle against the Japanese imperialists and Korean landlords, by their struggle for building a new life after Liberation and, especially, by the severe trials of the Fatherland Liberation War. The majority of entrepreneurs and traders, together with the entire people, not only took part in the democratic revolution after Liberation but also supported the policies pursued by our Party and the people's power in socialist construction. The Party's great prestige among the masses of the people, the rallying of people in all walks of life around the Party and the high political consciousness of the masses proved to be the most important guarantees for the successful implementation of socialist transformation.

As for socialist industrialization and modern farm machinery, it goes without saying that we cannot assure complete victory for socialism without developing industry further and equipping all branches of the national economy, including agriculture, with new techniques. However, socialist transformation could not be delayed when life itself demanded an immediate reorganization of the outdated relations of production and there were the revolutionary forces prepared to carry it out, even though the level of the productive forces and of technical progress was relatively low.

Our Party's policy was to assure rapid advance of the productive forces and, in particular, to open up a broad avenue for the technical revolution, by transforming, first and foremost, the relations of production along socialist lines in conformity with the matured requirements of social development, instead of waiting for industry to develop enough to carry out the technical reconstruction of the national economy. Only by transforming the relations of production could we restore rapidly and develop further the productive forces that had suffered severe war damage, and push forward the technical revolution vigorously and without delay in step with the development of industry.

When our Party advanced the task of all-round socialist transformation after the armistice, some argued that socialist transformation was "still premature," insisting that the revolution should not be pushed ahead any farther in the northern part of the country until the North and South were unified and the anti-imperialist, anti-feudal democratic revolution emerged victorious in the whole country. They considered that the socialist revolution in the North ran counter to the cause of unification of the country and was especially detrimental to the rallying of all the patriotic, democratic forces in South Korea in the anti-imperialist and anti-feudal struggle. They, of course, were wrong.

There is no reason whatever for North Korea to mark time because South Korea has not yet been liberated and the democratic revolution has not yet triumphed there. The socialist revolution and the building of socialism were raised not only as an irresistible demand of social development in the northern part of the country, but as a vital demand of the Korean revolution for consolidating the democratic base in the North, politically and economically. The most important guarantee for the victory of the Korean revolution is to eliminate the capitalist elements and root out all the foundations of counter-revolution in the North, building firm strongholds of socialism in town and country.

By mobilizing the masses our Party established a socialist system in the North and consolidated it in every way. Thus it has built this part of the country into the granite base of the Korean revolution, and turned it into a decisive force for accelerating the peaceful unification of the country. Today, the growth of the socialist forces and the free, happy life of the people under the socialist system in the North exert a tremendous revolutionary influence on all patriotic forces, including even the national bourgeoisie, not to speak of the workers and peasants, in South Korea, and inspire boundlessly the struggle of the people of South Korea against the U.S. imperialists and their henchmen.

Creatively applying the universal truth of Marxism-Leninism to our country's specific conditions, our Party, as I have mentioned above, raised in good time the tasks of socialist transformation in conformity with the matured requirements of social development, worked out a correct policy for their implementation, and carried through the policy with all firmness and consistency by mobilizing the masses, while overcoming Right and "Left" deviations of all descriptions.

Because the Party's policy of socialist transformation was correct and the masses, accepting it enthusiastically, were mobilized to carry it into effect with a high degree of revolutionary zeal, we could very smoothly accomplish in a short space of time the most complicated and difficult revolutionary tasks of transforming agriculture, handicrafts, and capitalist trade and industry along socialist lines, and establish the advanced, socialist system in the northern part of Korea.

THE CHOLLIMA MOVEMENT

The splendid achievements in socialist construction of our country have been scored in the midst of the great upsurge of socialist construction and in the course of the Chollima movement.*

The Chollima movement is a manifestation of the tremendous creative power of our people who have firmly rallied around the

---

*According to an ancient Korean legend, Chollima was a winged horse capable of carrying its rider at the speed of hundreds of miles a day toward "the land of happiness." The name was given to the movement launched in 1957 to fulfill the Five-Year Plan of industrialization ahead of time.

Party. It is a nationwide popular movement for the utmost acceleration of our socialist construction.

Our country had inherited a backward economy and culture from the old society and, in addition, went through a fierce war of three long years. We are building socialism in the conditions of north-south division of the country, standing face to face with the U.S. imperialists, and at the same time we are struggling for peaceful unification. In such a situation our struggle was bound to be exceedingly intense. Quickly to get rid of the backwardness left us by history, to accelerate the unification of the country, which is our supreme national task, we had to march ahead much faster than other people.

In view of this requirement of the development of our revolution, our Party mapped out a plan for definitely speeding up socialist construction in the North, and, on this basis, organized and mobilized the entire working people in the heroic struggle for socialist construction.

The working people of our country, educated and trained by the Party, were fully aware of the urgent requirements of the development of our revolution and of the historic mission they were entrusted with, and gave unanimous support to the Party's line of speeding up socialist construction.

In active response to the appeal of the Party, "Dash forward at the speed of Chollima!" our working people dashed ahead through thick and thin to carry out the task put forward by the Party. They rushed on and on, emulating each other, overcoming all obstacles and difficulties.

Thus, innovations were made and world-shaking miracles wrought almost every day on all fronts of socialist construction.

Our heroic working class built 300,000 to 400,000-ton-capacity blast furnaces, each in less than a year, laid a standard-gauge railway more than 80 kilometers in length in 75 days, and set up a huge, up-to-date vynalon* factory on a spot which had been only

---

*Vynalon is a synthetic fiber developed by Dr. Li Sung Gi; its basic raw material is limestone which is abundant in North Korea.

a waste land in a little over one year. Our working people turned out more than 13,000 extra machine tools over and above the state plan within a year by initiating the machine tool multiplying movement. Within a period of three to four months they erected over a thousand factories for local industry by utilizing idle material and manpower in local areas. They carried out in six months a tremendous job of remaking nature by irrigating 370,000 *jongbo** of paddy and dry fields. We can cite many such cases.

All these symbolize the heroic spirit and creative talent of our people who are rushing ahead at the speed of Chollima under the leadership of the Party.

Steadily advancing the Chollima movement, we have ensured the annual growth rate of industrial output at 30-40 per cent or even more, boosted our retarded farming in a short time and build anew cities and villages on their ruins.

The high tide of socialist construction and the Chollima movement in our country are a natural outcome of the great social and economic changes during the postwar period and of all the material and moral forces stored up by our Party and people in the course of their protracted, arduous struggle.

The definite victory of the socialist revolution and the creation of an independent economic foundation provided the social, economic and material conditions for the great upsurge in economic and cultural construction, creating the ground for the Chollima movement.

Objective conditions and possibilities alone, however, are not enough to bring forth the great upsurge in socialist construction. More decisive are our own forces, that is, the Party's ability to lead the masses in the revolutionary upsurge and the firm determination of the masses to carry through the will of the Party.

Through arduous struggles our Party has earned great prestige and trust among the masses and rallied them firmly around itself. The unbreakable unity of the Party's ranks and the establishment of Marxist-Leninist leadership throughout the Party increased its

---

*A *jongbo* equals a hectare, or 2.47 acres.

fighting capacity and greatly enhanced its prestige and influence among the masses. Thus, the will and ideas of the Party have always penetrated deep into the masses and become their own will and ideas.

Our people have accepted the Party's policies and line as a matter of vital interest to themselves and devoted their all to the struggle for the cause of revolution and for the prosperity and progress of their country. Previously deprived of power, our people seized and defended it with their blood. Formerly they were oppressed and humiliated, but now they are free from all exploitation and oppression. Therefore, it is only natural that they should display great revolutionary zeal to elevate their backward country, bringing it into the ranks of the advanced countries, and improve their difficult living conditions as early as possible.

Firmly counting on the high political enthusiasm and inexhaustible creative power of the working people, our Party has embarked on bold projects on all fronts of socialist construction and has vigorously carried them out.

In formulating its policy in each period of development of the revolution our Party not only had the present and the immediate future in mind but also scientifically foresaw the long-range prospects of the country's development and showed the masses the correct direction and a clear goal in their fight. Once a policy had been formulated, our Party never retreated in complex and difficult conditions. With unflagging tenacity it carried out its policy and line to the end.

Actively prompting the masses to maintain their high revolutionary zeal, our Party, having settled one problem, immediately posed the next for solution, thus kindling popular enthusiasm for continuous advance and uninterrupted innovations in all fields of socialist construction. At the same time, the Party correctly grasped the main link in each period of socialist construction and concentrated its efforts on it, thereby solving one problem after another and gaining full control of the whole chain of socialist construction.

The scientific foresight of the Party in formulating policy, its fidelity to Marxist-Leninist principle and its extraordinary revolutionary sweep in implementing policy always convinced the working people of the success of their work and made them advance unwaveringly toward the triumph of the great cause of socialism along the road illuminated by the Party.

The wise leadership of the Party, its firm unity with the people, their firm resolve to advance rapidly and their revolutionary zeal—these underlie the great upsurge in socialist construction and the Chollima movement and constitute the decisive guarantee for all our victories.

As Marxism-Leninism teaches us, the masses of the people are the creators of history. Socialism and communism can be built only by the conscious, creative labor of the toiling millions. Therefore, in socialist construction it is most important to arouse to the utmost the creative power of the masses and bring their enthusiasm, initiative and talent into full play. The great power of the Chollima movement lies in the very fact that it is a mass movement which gives full scope to the revolutionary zeal and creative talent of our people.

As is the case with all the innovation movements of the masses, the Chollima movement was born and has developed in the course of overcoming difficulties and obstacles, through the fight against the old. When socialist construction in our country entered a period of upsurge the main obstacles in rousing the revolutionary zeal and creative activity of the working people were passivism, conservatism and mystification of technique. Passivism and conservatism in socialist construction found expression in distrust of the might of our heroic working class and of the inexhaustible creative power and talent of our people. The passivists and conservatives tried to suppress the creativeness of the masses by clinging to old rated capacities and standards and by presenting science and technique as mysteries. Intimidated by difficulties and afraid of innovation, they attempted to arrest the grand onward movement of the masses. Without shattering passivism, conservatism and the mystification of technique, the great upsurge in socialist construction could not have been brought about, nor could the Chollima movement have been developed.

Our Party has fought a powerful ideological struggle among the cadres and working people against passivism and conservatism, and made tireless efforts to arm them with the revolutionary spirit of thinking boldly, acting boldly and making continuous advance and uninterrupted innovations. The Party has always believed in the great creative power of the masses and actively supported their bold suggestions and initiatives, rendering them every possible assistance to realize them in life. Boundlessly inspired by the correct leadership of the Party, our working people have smashed passivism and conservatism, courageously overcome all difficulties and achieved numerous feats of labor quite inconceivable in the past.

In promoting a high degree of labor enthusiasm and creative activity among the masses for socialist construction, it is very important incessantly to enhance their political and ideological consciousness, adequately combining it with the principle of material incentive.

Real mass labor upsurge can take place and real mass heroism can emerge in socialist construction only when the masses of the working people are armed firmly with the spirit of serving faithfully the Party and the revolution and with the spirit of selfless devotion to the country and the people. Unless the political awakening and the ideological level of the masses steadily are enhanced, a real communist attitude toward labor cannot be cultivated among them.

Under socialism, the political and moral stimulus to labor should always be backed by a material stimulus. Distribution according to the quality and quantity of work performed is an objective law in socialist society. It is a powerful means of opposing those who do not work and try to live at the expense of others, and of giving a material stimulus to the working people's enthusiasm for production.

Our Party consistently has taken the line of giving preference to political work in all activities and strengthening communist education among the working people so as to help them to display voluntary enthusiasm and devotion in labor, while strictly abiding by the socialist principle of distribution to stimulate their material interest in the results of their labor.

The correctness of this line finds vivid expression in the unprecedented labor upsurge among our working people. Today they are utilizing all their energies and talent for the benefit of the state and society, for their own happiness. Rapidly being fostered among them are the excellent communist traits of loving labor and regarding it as a matter of the highest honor, helping each other, working collectively and enjoying a happy life together.

The labor zeal and creative initiative of the masses can display their real power only when they are combined with science and technique. With the enthusiasm of the masses alone, devoid of advanced science and technique, we cannot go ahead far, nor can we make continuous innovations.

For the rapid development of science and technique, the broad masses of the working people should be enlisted actively in this work and creative cooperation should be strengthened between workers and peasants on the one hand and scientists and technicians on the other. We have smashed completely the wrong view that only one special category of people can develop science and technique, and have unfolded a mass movement among the working people for acquiring new techniques, inspiring them to constant technical innovations. In our technical progress we have fought resolutely the tendency to underestimate the creative proposals and initiatives of the workers and peasants and, at the same time, have strictly guarded against the tendency to ignore the significance of science and the role of scientists. We have always tried to combine labor and science and to promote close cooperation between workers and peasants on the one hand and scientists and technicians on the other. As the masses of the working people have come to possess science and technique, and as cooperation between workers and peasants on the one hand and scientists and technicians on the other has been strengthened, science and technique have developed still more speedily in our country and a collective technical renovation movement has been unfolded extensively in all fields of the national economy.

As a result, all the wisdom, talent, enthusiasm and creative power of our people, which were suppressed, trampled upon and buried in obscurity, have emerged into full flowering in the Chollima movement, effecting continuous innovations in economic and cultural construction.

The great political and economic significance of the Chollima movement lies first of all in the fact that it has brought about a high rate of socialist construction.

A high rate of economic growth is the rule in socialist society, and the planned and proportionate development of the national economy is a prerequisite for it. If the principles of planning and balancing are violated in economic development, it will bring about the waste of a tremendous amount of materials, funds and labor, and it will eventually retard general economic development, although certain branches may temporarily enjoy a high rate of growth.

The high rate of socialist construction in our country has been made possible on the basis of a planned and proportionate development of the national economy. Because of this the high rate of development could be maintained and all-round socialist construction accelerated even more throughout the Five-Year Plan period, to say nothing of the postwar rehabilitation period.

However high the rate of economic development may be, there will be no disproportion as long as the rate is based strictly on actual possibilities. Of course, it is very difficult to maintain due proportion while keeping up a very high rate. But, this rate should not be slackened to maintain a balance. Planning and balancing are not ends in themselves; they are a means for achieving a high rate of development. Hence, it is most important to rely on the advantages of the socialist system and the creative power of the masses and to utilize to the maximum the latent reserves and potentialities of the national economy so that all branches simultaneously can be developed at a rapid rate. In our socialist construction we always have calculated accurately material conditions and possibilities and, at the same time, had confidence in the revolutionary zeal and creative power of our people, tempered in arduous struggle. On this basis we have always drawn up active and bold plans and mobilized the masses for their fulfilment.

At the same time, our Party properly linked up and adequately coordinated the development of all branches of the national economy so as to boost promptly those which were lagging and prevent disproportions that might arise. Our Party made the year 1960 a period of adjustment. This was the most proper and judicious measure for securing an accurate proportion in the national economy and keeping up a high rate of development. In 1960, in some branches we eased the strain which had been caused in the course of rapid development and shored up certain lagging branches, while continuing to improve the material and cultural standards of the people. As a result, in all branches we fulfilled or overfulfilled the assignments under the Five-Year Plan, further consolidated our successes and made full preparations for the successful fulfillment of a new long-range plan. This has made it possible to maintain and extend the upsurge in socialist construction and continue the Chollima advance on a higher level.

Our Party found in the Chollima movement a definite guarantee for the successful building of socialism in our country. It has firmly taken the reins of this movement and developed it continuously in scope and depth.

The Chollima movement was developed still more after the completion of the socialist transformation of production relations and in the course of the all-Party struggle against the survivals of outdated ideas such as passivism, conservatism and mystification, in the course of the further intensification of communist education among the masses and the radical change of Party work into living, creative work with people.

Regarding it as the primary task in Pary work to educate and remold all people and unite them more firmly around itself, our Party in every way strengthened its work with people, and above all engaged in intensive communist education among the masses in combination with education in our revolutionary traditions. The Party's line of educating and remolding all people having been accepted by the masses, the remolding of people has become the work of the masses themselves, and has been linked more closely with their productive activities.

The main feature of the Chollima work-team movement,* now spreading rapidly among our working people, lies in the close combination of the mass innovation drive in production with the education and remolding of workers.

This work-team movement, as an intensified and higher form of the Chollima movement, has become not only a powerful impetus to the development of the national economy and an ideal form of mass economic management by the working people, but also constitutes an excellent medium of mass education for remolding everybody into a person of a new, communist type. Our Chollima riders are not only innovators in production, but also able management personnel, expert organizers and real communist educators.

In our country at present, the Chollima work-team movement is going on in all fields of industry, agriculture, transport, construction, science, education, culture, public health, and so forth, and the ranks of the Chollima riders, the heroes of our age, are growing day after day. As of the end of August this year, upwards of two million working people had joined this movement; 4,958 work-teams and workshops, involving 125,028 persons, have received the title of Chollima, and 55 work-teams with 1,459 persons have been honored with it twice, becoming Double Chollima work-teams.

Thus, the Chollima movement has become a great revolutionary movement of the working millions of our country, sweeping

---

*The work-team movement, initiated on the suggestion of Kim Il Sung at the Kangson Steel works in 1959, developed rapidly into a higher stage of the Chollima movement. The first national conference of Chollima Work-Team Riders was held in August 1960. (For a full description *see* Kim Byong Sik, *Modern Korea,* New York, 1970.)

away all that is antiquated from every sphere of economy and culture, ideology and morality, making constant innovations and accelerating socialist construction at an unprecedented rate. The movement has become our Party's general line in socialist construction.

The essence of this line is to unite the entire working people more closely around our Party by educating and remolding them in communist ideology, bringing their revolutionary zeal and creative talent into full play, so that socialism can be built faster and better. The indestructible vitality of this line lies in the fact that it was initiated by the masses themselves, that it is a line the Party advanced by reflecting the will of the masses and generalizing their experience of struggle, and that the masses have therefore accepted it wholeheartedly.

On the strength of this line our Party has won great victories in socialist construction, and following this line it will achieve still greater victories.

III.

THE RURAL QUESTION UNDER SOCIALISM
Basic Principles

THE RURAL question presents itself in a different light at different stages of the development of the revolution.

In the stage of the anti-imperialist, anti-feudal democratic revolution the peasant and agricultural questions consisted in emancipating the peasantry from exploitation and enslavement by the landlords, and in freeing the productive forces of agriculture from the fetters of the feudal relations of production through the abolition of feudal landownership in the countryside. We solved these questions successfully by carrying out land reform in a thorough-going way, on the principle of confiscating the landlords' land and distributing it to the peasants without compensation.

In the stage of the socialist revolution the peasant and agricultural questions consist in emancipating the peasantry once and for all from every kind of exploitation and oppression, and in completely freeing the productive forces of agriculture from the fetters of the old production relations based on private ownership by liquidating the capitalist elements in the countryside and reorganizing the private peasant economy into a socialist collective economy. We have solved these questions with credit by carrying out the socialist cooperativization of agriculture through

From *Theses on the Socialist Rural Question in Our Country.* Adopted at the Eighth Plenary meeting of the Fourth Central Committee of the Workers Party of Korea, February 25, 1964.

teaching by example and with the application of the voluntary principle, under the strong leadership and with the active assistance of the Party and the state.

The socialist system of agriculture enjoys decisive superiority over the private peasant economy and the capitalist system of agriculture. It opens up a broad avenue for the development of the productive forces in agriculture and offers possibilities for the rapid improvement of the material and cultural life of the peasantry.

The question is how to conduct rural work and how to develop the rural economy under the socialist system.

After the triumph of the socialist system in town and country the rural question presents itself in a fundamentally different light than in the preceding periods.

Under socialism the peasant and agricultural questions become a matter of developing the productive forces of agriculture to a high level, making the life of the peasants a bountiful one, abolishing the backwardness of the countryside left over by the exploiter society, and gradually obliterating the distinctions between town and country, on the basis of the continuous strengthening of the socialist system established in the countryside.

Among the most fundamental tasks in building socialism and preparing for the transition to communism is the gradual elimination of the distinctions between town and country, while consolidating and developing the socialist system of agriculture. This complicated and difficult task can be completely solved only by protracted and unremitting struggle and effort.

With the completion of socialist transformation, this task has already been placed on the order of the day in our country. Our work in the rural areas should proceed in the direction of solving this problem.

For the successful solution of the peasant and agricultural questions under socialism, it is imperative to adhere firmly to three basic principles in rural work.

First, the technical, cultural and ideological revolutions should be carried out thoroughly in the rural areas.

Second, leadership of the peasantry by the working class, assistance of industry to agriculture, and support of the towns to the countryside should be strengthened in every way.

Third, the guidance and management of the rural economy should steadily be brought closer to the advanced level of management of industrial enterprises, the links between ownership by the whole people and cooperative ownership should be strengthened, and cooperative ownership should constantly be brought closer to ownership by the whole people.

1. THE TECHNICAL, CULTURAL AND IDEOLOGICAL REVOLUTIONS

The revolution must be continued to achieve the full-scale construction of socialism and to prepare for the gradual transition to communism.

The very fact that the distinctions between town and country and the class distinction between the working class and the peasantry remain even after the liquidation of the exploiting classes and the completion of socialist transformation shows that the revolution should be carried forward and that the revolution in the rural areas, in particular, should be carried out more thoroughly. Should the revolution be halted because socialist cooperativization has been achieved, the enthusiasm of the peasants, which has been heightened by the democratic and socialist revolutions, cannot be maintained and increased. Without continuing the revolution in the countryside, the socialist system in agriculture cannot be consolidated and developed, nor can its advantages be displayed or the distinctions between town and country be eliminated.

The technical, cultural and ideological revolutions are the central revolutionary tasks that must be accomplished in the rural areas following the completion of socialist cooperativization.

The lag of the farm villages behind the towns finds its expression, first of all, in the fact that agriculture has a weaker material and technical foundation than industry, that the cultural level of the rural population is lower than that of the city dwellers, and that the peasants lag behind the workers in thinking and consciousness. Needless to say, this backwardness is a legacy of the old society, and the fact that it still remains under socialism likewise is connected, in a large measure, with the level of development of industry and of the towns. Precisely due to this backwardness, cooperative ownership remains the dominant form in agriculture, in contrast with industry where ownership by the whole people prevails, and as a result the class distinction between the working class and the peasantry remains.

Therefore, in order to consolidate and develop the socialist system of agriculture, to eliminate the distinctions between town and country, and to eliminate the class distinction between the working class and the peasantry, the three revolutions—technical, cultural and ideological—must, first of all, be carried out in the countryside on the basis of the rapid development of socialist industry and of the towns, thus overcoming the backwardness of the countryside in all three spheres.

The tasks of the technical, cultural and ideological revolutions in the countryside are closely inter-linked and they must be carried out as a unified process.

Among them, the ideological revolution is the most important and most difficult, and it must be stressed above all other work. It would be a grave error to put the accent on the technical and cultural revolutions alone and neglect the ideological revolution.

The class struggle continues also under socialism. The class struggle in the socialist countryside finds expression in the struggle against the subversive machinations of the hostile elements infiltrating from outside and of the remnants of the overthrown exploiting classes, and also in the ideological struggle against the survivals of obsolete ideas in the minds of the peasants. Unless the class consciousness of the peasants is raised and the ideological struggle is intensified among them, the socialist system cannot be consolidated in the countryside, nor can it be safeguarded from enemy encroachment.

The advantages of socialism and its vitality lie, above all, in the fact that under this system the working people who have been freed from exploitation and oppression are solidly united, co-operate closely with each other in a comradely way, and do their work voluntarily and enthusiastically for the common goal and interests. Without raising the peasants' level of thinking and consciousness, these intrinsic advantages of socialism cannot be demonstrated in the countryside, nor, in consequence, can farm production, agricultural technique and rural culture be advanced rapidly.

The remolding of the peasants' thinking and consciousness does not come of itself with the establishment of the socialist system and improvement of living conditions. It goes without saying that with the triumph of the socialist system, the economic foundation generating obsolete ideas disappears and the social and material conditions for equipping the peasants with new ideology are created. But under socialism, too, the residue of obsolete ideas, and particularly petty-proprietor inclinations, persist for a long time in the minds of the peasants, and may revive and even grow when ideological work is slackened. The thinking and consciousness of the peasants can be remolded completely only by prolonged, tireless education and constant struggle.

Attaching primary importance to the ideological revolution does not in any way mean that we may neglect the technical and cultural revolutions.

Socialism and communism require a high level of development of the productive forces as well as a high cultural level among the working people. The aim of building socialism and communism is, in the final analysis, to assure a happy life for the entire people and to satisfy more fully their steadily growing material and cultural needs.

There can be neither development of the agricultural productive forces, nor improvement in the material and cultural standards of the peasants, nor emancipation of the peasants from heavy toil, unless the technical and cultural revolutions are carried out in the countryside. The reinforcement of the material and technical basis of agriculture and the elevation of the peasants' cultural level are also important requisites for remolding the thoughts and consciousness of the peasants. Hence, to stress only the importance of the ideological revolution, while neglecting the technical and cultural revolutions, is likewise an error.

While giving decisive priority to the ideological revolution, we must promote energetically the technical and cultural revolutions along with it. In this way we must recast the ideology of the peasants, reinforce the material and technical basis of agriculture and raise the cultural level of the rural population.

2. WORKING-CLASS LEADERSHIP OF THE PEASANT-RY, ASSISTANCE OF INDUSTRY TO AGRICULTURE, AND SUPPORT OF THE TOWN TO THE COUNTRYSIDE

Leadership and assistance by the Party and the state of the working class are indispensable conditions for the emergence, consolidation and development of the socialist system in the countryside. The peasantry can take the socialist path and then go over to communism only under the leadership and with the assistance of the working class.

The workers and peasants are allies fighting together for the common goal and ideal; they are all socialist working people. Ownership by the whole people and cooperative ownership are the two forms of socialist ownership that develop hand in hand and they constitute the economic foundations of the socialist state. The socialist state assumes responsibility for the livelihood not only of the factory and office workers but also of the peasants; it assumes responsibility for the development not only of ownership by the whole people but also of cooperative ownership. In the days of the private peasant economy, each peasant was chiefly responsible for his own husbandry and livelihood. But after the completion of cooperativization, the Party and the state should bear responsibility for and look after the development of the cooperative farms and the peasants' livelihood.

Industry is the leading department of the people's economy, and the towns are ahead of the countryside in all spheres of politics, economy and culture. Agriculture can become as well equipped with modern techniques as industry only when industry, the leading department, gives it assistance, and the lagging countryside can attain the level of the towns only when the latter, which are ahead, give it support.

From this it follows that in order vigorously to promote the technical, cultural and ideological revolutions in the countryside and eliminate gradually the distinctions between town and country after the completion of socialist cooperativization, the Party and the state should strengthen in every way their leadership of and assistance to the rural areas, and the towns should give active support to the countryside.

Needless to say, in a formerly backward agrarian country like ours, the rural areas have to provide a certain amount of funds for socialist industrialization for a certain period following the victory of the revolution. The supplying of funds by the peasants for the creation of a modern socialist industry benefits the whole of society, and it is also indispensable for the future development of agriculture and improvement of the living conditions of the peasants themselves.

But once the foundation of socialist industry has been laid, the emphasis should be shifted, industry now coming to the aid of agriculture. From that time on, agriculture should be given ever more powerful and all-round assistance.

The working class must not only lead the peasantry politically and ideologically, but must also give it material, technical, cultural and financial assistance. The socialist state must make every effort to lighten the burdens of the peasants and increase their income, and must see to it that the living standards of the workers and peasants rise evenly in relation to each other.

Should rural work be neglected, should the rural areas be left without aid or, worse still, should there be industrial development alone at the expense of agriculture and urban construction alone at the sacrifice of the countryside, then the discrepancy between town and country, far from disappearing, will grow ever greater. This will make it impossible to give full play to the activity of the peasants, develop agriculture or improve the peasants' living standards. It will, in the long run, hinder the development of industry itself, as well as that of the whole people's economy and cause severe damage to the building of socialism and communism.

It is a capitalist idea to neglect the countryside. Under capitalism it is the rule that the towns exploit the countryside and the latter lags behind the former.

Communists decisively reject the idea of neglecting the countryside and from the first day of their coming to power they should strive to rid the countryside of backwardness, a legacy of capitalism. Under socialism it is law-given that the towns assist the countryside and that the once backward countryside approaches ever closer to the level of the towns in all spheres.

While increasing the strength of the working class and continuing to develop industry and the towns, we must strengthen constantly working-class leadership of the peasantry, and increase assistance by industry to agriculture and support by the towns for the countryside, thereby diminishing step by step the distinctions between town and country. Only in this way can we continue to give full play to the active role of the peasants, rapidly develop the rural economy and better the peasants' livelihood. This will eventually lend a greater impetus to the development of industry itself, and to that of the whole people's economy, and accelerate the building of socialism and communism.

3. GUIDANCE AND MANAGEMENT OF AGRICULTURE, RELATION BETWEEN OWNERSHIP BY THE WHOLE PEOPLE AND COOPERATIVE OWNERSHIP

Under socialism, the countryside lags behind the towns not only in the technical, cultural and ideological spheres, but also, and as a result, in its form of ownership and level of economic management. The difference between industry and agriculture in respect of ownership is an essential one that determines the class distinction between the working class and the peasantry. The difference between industry and agriculture in their level of economic management is also a major factor.

Therefore, in order to eliminate the distinctions between town and country and the class distinction between the working class and the peasantry, it is necessary to rid the countryside of backwardness in technique, culture and ideology, and also in ownership and the level of economic management. Only by so doing can the lag of the rural areas behind the towns be overcome completely, all distinctions between town and country connected with that lag be eliminated, and the class distinction between the working class and the peasantry be overcome.

For the elimination of the distinctions between industry and agriculture in the level of economic management and ownership, it is necessary to promote energetically the technical, cultural and ideological revolutions in the countryside, strengthening in every way the support of the towns for the rural areas, and on this basis improve the guidance and management of the rural economy and gradually bring cooperative ownership up to the level of ownership by the whole people. Meanwhile, the improvement of guidance and management of the rural economy, development of cooperative ownership, and maintenance of a correct correlation between ownership by the whole people and cooperative ownership constitute important requisites for the acceleration of the technical, cultural and ideological revolutions in the rural areas, for effective assistance by the towns to the countryside, and for the successful solution of all problems involved in building the socialist countryside.

The basic direction in improving the guidance and management of socialist agriculture consists in steadily bringing the method of management in the agricultural cooperative economy closer to the more advanced method of management of industrial enterprises.

The agricultural cooperative economy is a large-scale socialist economy that is being equipped rapidly with modern technique. Inasmuch as the scale of management in agriculture is expanding and agriculture gradually is approaching the level of industry in its technical equipment, the method of guidance and management of agriculture should also be brought closer to the method of management of industrial enterprises. This means, above all, that the industrial method of management must be employed in guiding and managing the agricultural cooperative economy.

Management by the industrial method means the strengthening of technical guidance in production and the planning and systematization of all management work in an enterprise. Agriculture lags behind industry in technical equipment, and still more in technical guidance. Planning and systematization have been introduced in the management of agriculture since the cooperativization of the private peasant economy. But in this respect, too, agriculture lags far behind industry.

Intensified technical guidance and increased planning and systematization of all management work—this is the basic direction in improving the management of the agricultural cooperative economy and in eliminating the lag of agriculture behind industry in economic management.

Employment of the industrial method of management in the agricultural cooperative economy will render it possible to accelerate the technical revolution in the countryside, overcome desultoriness and lack of organization in the management of agriculture, make rational use of land, farm machines and other means of production as well as of labor power, and improve practices in farm production. It will give a strong impetus to the increase of agricultural production, the consolidation of the cooperative economy and the improvement of the peasants' livelihood.

The problem of the development of cooperative ownership and of the correlation between ownership by the whole people (in industry) and cooperative ownership (in agriculture) is one of the basic problems in building the socialist countryside and in socialist construction as a whole. This is an issue of principle, having a direct bearing on the social and economic position of the peasants and on the relationship between the working class and the peasantry.

The system of cooperative economy, which is dominant in agriculture, conforms to the nature and level of the productive forces and the level of development of the peasants' consciousness under socialism. The system of cooperative economy in agriculture, displaying its immense superiority, gives a powerful stimulus to the development of the productive forces. For the speedy development of socialist agriculture, it is necessary to mobilize and turn to maximum account the potentialities and possibilities of the system of cooperative economy.

This, however, does not at all mean that under socialism the system of cooperative economy in agriculture will remain immutable. Cooperative ownership develops and changes, too. It is necessary that cooperative ownership be developed and perfected in keeping with the strengthening of the material and technical basis of the rural economy and the rise in the peasants' level of culture, thinking and consciousness.

At the same time, the questions of the correlation between ownership by the whole people and cooperative ownership, the ties between industry and agriculture, must be solved correctly. What is of prime importance in this connection is organically to link the two types of ownership in such a way as to strengthen the direct ties between industry and agriculture in production and constantly enhance the leading role of ownership by the whole people over cooperative ownership.

For this purpose, it is necessary to reinforce the state enterprises which serve the rural economy directly—the farm-machine stations, irrigation control offices, seed farms and seed-treatment centers, experimental farms, stock-breeding farms and epizootic prevention centers—and to enlist the active participation of these enterprises in agricultural production at the cooperative farms. These state enterprises must be placed on solid material and technical foundations and be managed in an exemplary way, and their role in the development of cooperative farming be constantly increased. As industry develops, they must be expanded and steadily reinforced so that the modern material and technical means owned by the whole people will gradually account for an overwhelming proportion of agricultural production.

Only by closely linking ownership by the whole people with cooperative ownership is it possible for the working class to increase its political and ideological influence on the peasantry, for industry to introduce more successfully into agriculture its machine technology, advanced methods of industrial management and modern practices in production, and for the town to give effective assistance to the countryside. Only by so doing can we consolidate and develop cooperative ownership and bring it closer to ownership by the whole people, and only then can we facilitate and accelerate the process of gradual transition from cooperative ownership to ownership by the whole people. This is the way to elevate the leading role of the working class and to strengthen further the worker-peasant alliance, accelerating the building of socialism and communism.

If we were to take the course of weakening the leading role of ownership by the whole people over cooperative ownership and of separating the two, it would weaken the political and ideological influence of the working class upon the peasantry, render it impossible for industry to introduce successfully into agriculture its machine technology, advanced methods of industrial management and modern practices in production, and hinder the town from giving support to the countryside. If things were to go that way, the system of socialist agriculture could not be consolidated and developed, nor could the gradual transition from cooperative ownership to ownership by the whole people be effected successfully. Such a course would, in the long run, lower the leading role of the working class and weaken the worker-peasant alliance, and would place difficulties in the way of socialist and communist construction.

It is also wrong to convert cooperative ownership into ownership by the whole people in a hurry, in disregard of actual conditions and possibilities. Should cooperative ownership be converted into ownership by the whole people at a time when the material and technical foundations of agriculture are still weak, when big differences still exist between industrial and agricultural labor, and the peasantry lags behind the working class in the level of ideas, consciousness and culture, that would only result in retarding the development of the socialist countryside and socialist construction as a whole.

While constantly enhancing the leading role of ownership by the whole people over cooperative ownership, we should organically link the two types of ownership, and thereby consolidate and develop our system of socialist agriculture and bring cooperative ownership closer to ownership by the whole people. By creating the actual conditions and possibilities in this way, we must convert cooperative ownership gradually into ownership by the whole people.

IV.

ON THE UNIFICATION
OF KOREA

January 8,1965,
Pyongyang, Korea

Mr. Yongjeung Kim, President
Korean Affairs Institute,
2907 Ellicot Street,
Washington 8, D.C., U.S.A.

I have received your letter. It gives me great pleasure to know that you are deeply concerned with the question of unification of the country.

As you know, our nation has been suffering from territorial partition and national split for the past twenty years.

A new generation has grown up, yet not even contact and travel between North and South Korea have been realized, to say nothing of the unification of the country, the long-cherished aspiration of the nation; and the artificial barrier of the national split still remains.

As the days go by, the gap between the North and the South is widening further in all spheres of political, economic and cultural life, and even the national features common to our people, a homogeneous nation formed during a long history, are gradually becoming differentiated.

The splitting of the nation rules out the possibility of mobilizing

---

Reply to the letter of the President of the Korean Affairs Institute in Washington.

and using the wealth of the country and the strength of the people in a unified way for the development of the country, and it brings unbearable sufferings to the entire Korean people.

The division of Korea into the North and the South brings immeasurable misfortunes and disasters, particularly to the life of the people in South Korea.

The prosperity of the whole nation cannot be expected nor can the South Korean people be rescued from the quagmire unless the splitting of the country is overcome and unification is achieved.

It is natural that today, in South Korea, the broad masses of the people are crying out that they cannot live without the unification of the country, and many public figures with national conscience are fighting courageously for the unification of the country.

The unification of the country is an urgent national task that brooks no further delay.

It is high time, we think, that all Koreans without exception, who love the country and are concerned about the future of the nation, do their utmost for the unification of the country.

As is widely known to the world, our Government, reflecting the unanimous desire and will of the entire Korean people, has made persevering efforts to achieve the unification of the country.

We consider that the solution of the unification question should not be hampered in the interests of a certain grouping or privileged circles at the expense of national interests; we consider that unification should be accomplished in a democratic way in accordance with the general will of the entire Korean people, and not, under any circumstances, by one side forcing its will on the other side. We do not allow anyone to impose his will upon us and we, on our part, do not intend to force our will on others. We always maintain that the authorities, political parties, public organizations and public figures of North and South Korea should sit around one table and negotiate sincerely and with an open heart to solve the question of unification.

I make it clear once again that our Government will, as always, bend all efforts toward realizing the unification of the country in conformity with the desire of the people and the national interests and will be ready to accept the opinion of anyone, provided it is helpful for the solution of the unification question.

In your letter you set forth views that have many points in common with a number of proposals we have outlined time and again for the settlement of the question of unifying the country.

As we have always maintained, the unification of the country should and must be realized on the principles of independence and democracy, in a peaceful way, without any interference from outside.

We consider that any attempt to accomplish the unification of the country by relying upon outside forces is a mere illusion and is designed to leave the whole of Korea to the imperialist aggressors.

The question of Korea's unification is an internal affair of the Korean people, in which no outside force is permitted to interfere. The Korean question must be settled by the Koreans themselves. Foreigners are not in a position to solve the internal affairs of our nation.

Our nation is a resourceful and civilized nation with adequate ability to solve its own national problem by itself.

The basic obstacle to the country's unification is U.S. imperialism which, militarily occupying South Korea, interferes in the domestic affairs of our country, carries out the policy of splitting our nation and pursues an aggressive policy against the whole of Korea.

The U.S. imperialists have brought South Korea completely under their colonial domination in all political, economic, military and cultural fields and have completely ruined the livelihood of the people there.

Withdrawal of all foreign troops from South Korea is the precondition for the solution of the question of unification.

In North Korea there are no foreign troops whatever. The Chinese People's Volunteers withdrew completely from North Korea on their own initiative as early as 1958.

However, the U.S. army in the guise of the United Nations is still stationed in South Korea.

The United States has no ground or excuse whatsoever to station its army in South Korea.

There can be no independence or sovereignty as long as a foreign army of aggression is stationed in one's territory.

All people with even an ounce of national conscience should demand the withdrawal of the U.S. troops and strive to expel them from our territory.

We must kindle nationwide wrath against the U.S. imperialist aggressors and marshal all the patriotic forces in the struggle for driving the U.S. Army out of South Korea.

Your proposal that all foreign troops should be withdrawn for the solution of the question of Korea's unification is just.

It is our consistent view that the question of Korea's unification should be solved through the establishment of a unified central government embracing the representatives of the people of all strata by free general elections in both the North and the South to be held in a democratic way, free from any interference by outside force, after the withdrawal of all the foreign troops from South Korea.

Such general elections should be held in a completely free and democratic atmosphere, without any conditions that might hamper or repress, even to the slightest degree, the expression of the will of the people. Free, democratic elections are unthinkable as long as the democratic rights of the people are infringed upon and patriotic movements are suppressed.

For free North-South general elections, first of all, complete freedom of political activity for all political parties, public organizations and public figures as well as freedom of speech, the press, assembly, association and demonstration should be fully guaranteed in the whole area of North and South Korea. All political offenders who have been arrested and imprisoned for having demanded democratic freedom and the unification of the country by the Koreans themselves should be set free unconditionally.

All citizens should be entitled to vote and to be elected throughout Korea, with equal rights, irrespective of party affiliation, political views, property status, education, religious faith, or sex.

Only through such genuine democratic elections based on the principles of universal, equal and direct suffrage by secret ballot, can an independent, democratic, unified government representing the interests of workers, peasants, youth and students, intellectuals, servicemen, traders, entrepreneurs and other people of all strata be established.

This proposal of ours is most fair and reasonable and should be acceptable to anyone.

However, the successive rulers of South Korea, doggedly opposing this just proposal of ours, have insisted on "U.N.-supervised elections."

The Korean people are well aware of the nature of "U.N.-supervised elections." It is no secret that the election of Syngman Rhee, traitor to the Korean people, was rigged several times, Chang Myon's assumption of power was fabricated, and seizure of power by Pak Jung Hi* was legalized through so-called "U.N.-supervised elections" imposed on South Korea from 1948 to this date.

"U.N.-supervised elections" are no more than a screen for covering the aggressive plots of the U.S. imperialists to extend to North Korea their colonial system which they have forced upon the South Korean people.

In Korea the United Nations has been used as an aggressive tool by the United States.

The United Nations has no competence whatsoever to have a part in the Korean question.

The Korean people have no need for anyone's interference in solving the question of the unification of their country. We must by all means achieve the unification of the country on our own.

---

*As a result of the April Popular Uprising (1960), Syngman Rhee was replaced by Chang Myon in an effort to appease popular unrest; in May 1961 a military coup placed in power General Pak Jung Hi (referred to in the American press as "President Chung Hee Park").

Since the South Korean authorities kept on opposing, at the instigation of U.S. imperialism, the establishment of a unified government of Korea through free, democratic elections, we could not merely sit with folded arms waiting for the day of the country's unification nor could we refrain from seeking ways and means for a gradual approach to complete unification by taking all measures beneficial to the unification of the country.

You must know that we have long since proposed the establishment of a North-South Confederation as a transitional step toward settling the urgent and immediate problems of the nation, even before the accomplishment of complete unification, and toward promoting its unification.

The Confederation we have proposed envisages the setting up of a supreme national committee composed of equal numbers of representatives appointed by the two governments mainly for coordinating the economic and cultural development of North and South Korea in a uniform way and for promoting mutual cooperation and interchange for the common interests of the nation, while retaining the existing political systems in North and South Korea and maintaining the independent activities of the two governments.

The unification commission you have recommended may be regarded as similar to the supreme national committee we proposed. Measures may also be sought for re-establishing national ties between the North and the South and realizing the unification of the country independently, not necessarily through the form of a confederate system, but by setting up a joint body in some other form, composed of representatives of North and South Korea.

We have proposed time and again that if the South Korean authorities cannot accept that Confederation, the nation's tribulations caused by the division should be lessened even a little by effecting North-South economic and cultural interchange, leaving aside political questions for the time being.

Economic exchange between the North and the South will combine organically industry in North Korea with agriculture in South Korea and facilitate the uniform, independent development of the national economy, revive the ruined South Korean economy, and open the door for improving the living conditions of the South Korean people, who are in a dire plight.

We have already built a developed industry and agriculture in North Korea and laid the firm economic foundation of an independent state. This provides the economic wherewithal for our nation to live by its own means when the country is unified at a future date.

When we rebuilt the economy utterly devastated by the U.S. imperialist aggressors, tightening our belts, we were at all times mindful of the interests and future development of the whole nation. We have not forgotten our compatriots in South Korea even for a moment; we consider it our sacred national duty to help the suffering people in South Korea.

Along with the realization of economic interchange, cultural ties covering the spheres of science, culture, arts, sports, etc., should be restored, and mutual visits between the North and the South should be undertaken.

The South Korean authorities, following at the heels of U.S. imperialism, are opposed to free North-South general elections, opposed to a confederation of North and South Korea and opposed even to economic and cultural exchange and mutual visits between the North and the South.

Under these circumstances, we called for the resumption of correspondence as the minimum measure to establish ties between the North and the South. It reflects the pressing demand of the people for the elimination of the extremely abnormal situation in which parents, wives and children, relatives and friends separated in the North and the South cannot even write to each other.

It is of primary importance in achieving the unification of the country to eliminate the tension created between the North and the South.

In this connection, it might be recalled, we have time and again proposed to the South Korean authorities that the U.S. troops be withdrawn completely from South Korea, that the North and

South Korean authorities conclude a peace agreement pledging not to resort to armed attack against each other, and that the armed forces of North and South Korea be reduced to 100,000 or less, respectively.

The oversized armed forces of South Korea, numbering more than 600,000, are imposing an unbearably heavy burden of military expenditure upon the South Korean people and seriously menacing peace in Korea.

The withdrawal of all foreign troops from South Korea, the conclusion of a peace agreement between the North and the South and the reduction of the armed forces of the two parts will mark a giant step forward for unification of the country.

We welcome your proposal that the North and South Korean armies be cut to the level of constabulary units solely for the maintenance of security and order in the country.

We will take any other measure beneficial to the solution of the question of unification. We are ready to abrogate the military pacts we have concluded with foreign countries on condition that the U.S. Army is withdrawn from South Korea and the South Korean authorities abolish all the military pacts and agreements they have concluded with foreign countries. We made this clear at the time we were concluding our pacts with other countries.

Our regime is an independent people's regime established freely in accordance with the general will of the people. We have never relied upon outside forces and we maintain complete independence in all spheres—politics, economy, military, culture, etc.

Our home and foreign policies are completely independent policies rejecting any interference by foreign countries. Whenever necessary, our Government can take, on its own initiative, appropriate measures for the interests of the country and the nation.

We have shown all sincerity in the effort to achieve unification of the country.

Even after the present rulers of South Korea staged a military coup and seized power, we have repeatedly advanced a number of proposals of national salvation, for overcoming the national calamity and accelerating the unification of the country, in the sincere hope that they would return to a national stand.

They, however, trailing behind the aggressive and splitting policy of the U.S. imperialists and disregarding the ardent desire of the nation, have refused to give ear to our sincere advice; on the contrary, they persist in perpetuating the national split.

The responsibility for the failure up to now to achieve the unification of our country rests with the U.S. imperialists who have occupied South Korea by armed might and have been enforcing a policy of splitting our nation and with such traitors as Pak Jung Hi, the reactionary bureaucrats, the political mountebanks and impostors who, hand in glove with the U.S. imperialists, are bartering away the interests of the nation.

It is they who serve the foreign aggressive forces, opposing the peaceful independent unification of the country and categorically rejecting the unity of all national forces, and it is they who defend only their own personal interests and the interests of some privileged circles in league with outside forces, but can never represent the South Korean people.

They are making excuses for the U.S. aggressive army which has occupied South Korea and has been hampering the unification of our country and perpetrating all sorts of bestial atrocities against the South Korean people, such as plundering, oppressing, insulting and killing, and are asking for its permanent stationing there.

These traitors turned down our offer to take millions of South Korean unemployed into North Korea to give them jobs, and are shipping out our compatriots to European and American countries like a commodity.

Moreover, they are even encouraging the Japanese militarists to turn South Korea into a dual colony of the U.S. and Japanese imperialists.

Manipulated by the United States, the traitors of South Korea, who are dead set against contact and cooperation with one and the same nation, are working hard to bring the criminal "South

Korea-Japan talks" to completion for the purpose of collusion with the Japanese militarists.

Those taking the lead in collusion with Japanese imperialism are the lackeys who also faithfully served it in the past. Refusing to reflect on their past crimes, today they have become the cat's paws of U.S. imperialism and their old master, Japanese militarism.

To achieve the unification of the country, we should fight, pooling the strength of the entire people in North and South Korea, against the foreign imperialist aggressive forces and the traitors, the reactionary bureaucrats, political mountebanks and impostors who in league with these forces are hampering unification.

How can we promote national unity and achieve the unification of the country without fighting against those who, far from being desirous of unification, are categorically rejecting any contact or interchange between the North and the South?

Needless to say, it would be a different matter if they were to repent of their mistakes even now and take the road of struggle for the withdrawal of the U.S. Army and for the independent unification of the country.

We will join hands with anyone at any time if he defends the interest of the nation and aspires to the country's unification, irrespective of his political views and ideology and of his past actions.

If all the patriotic forces of North and South Korea unite we will surely be able to open the road of contact and negotiation between the North and the South, achieve mutual cooperation and interchange, compel the U.S. Army to withdraw, and accomplish the unification of the country.

Without unity and struggle we can neither drive out the U.S. aggressive army nor achieve the unification of the country.

The point is that the South Korean people from all walks of life—workers, peasants, youth, students, intellectuals, army men, traders and entrepreneurs—should firmly unite and wage a more resolute national-salvation struggle for the peaceful, independent unification of the country against U.S. imperialism and its lackeys.

We must not allow any form of intereference in the domestic affairs of our nation, must thoroughly oppose "protection" or "supervision" by any one, and must carve out our own destiny by ourselves.

When we achieve the unification of our country on the principle of national self-determination and the whole nation unites in a common struggle, we will be able to strengthen the might of the country and build a rich and powerful independent sovereign state, dispensing with "guarantees" by any outside forces.

Our country will certainly be united by the nationwide struggle of the entire Korean people.

In conclusion, I hope you will make positive efforts to accelerate the independent unification of the country.

KIM IL SUNG
Premier of the Cabinet, Democratic People's Republic of Korea

V.

SOCIALIST CONSTRUCTION

ECONOMIC CONSTRUCTION

ECONOMIC CONSTRUCTION is a very important task for the Marxist-Leninist Party which has assumed power.

Once in power, the Marxist-Leninist Party must be responsible for the life of the people and is duty-bound systematically to improve their material and cultural well-being. The question of the people's livelihood can be solved only when economic construction is done well. Also, economic construction creates material conditions for strengthening the might of the country and for consolidating the victories already gained in the revolution and further expanding and developing them. Economic construction in the northern half of our country, in particular, is of decisive significance not only for the happy life of the people there, but also for the strengthening of our revolutionary base, the guarantee of the unification of the fatherland, and for assisting the people of South Korea in their revolutionary struggle. Our Party, therefore, ever since the early days of Liberation, has made every effort to consolidate the economic foundations of the country and steadily improve the people's livelihood.

In our country, which was formerly under imperialist colonial rule, the most important question in socialist economic construction was to create and develop a modern industry.

In the years of Japanese imperialist rule our industry was insignificant. Owing to the exclusive sway of Japanese imperialist capital, the development of national industry was severely re-

From *Socialist Construction in the Democratic People's Republic of Korea and the South Korean Revolution,* Lecture at the Ali Archam Academy of Social Sciences of Indonesia, April 14, 1965.

stricted and even the traditional handicrafts were totally ruined. With the sole aim of plundering Korea of her resources and exploiting her people, the Japanese imperialists built in our country only a few industries producing raw materials and semi-finished goods. The manufacturing industries were quite negligible, and machine-building in particular was practically non-existent. The technical equipment of industry was extremely backward.

It was this colonial industry which we inherited from the old society, and even that was utterly destroyed owing to the war.

In these circumstances, a modern industry could not be built merely by rehabilitating and developing the industry which already existed. We had to put an end to the colonial lopsidedness of our industry and radically improve its technical equipment, while ensuring a high rate of growth in industrial output.

On the basis of the nationalization of the key industries which was effected immediately after Liberation, our Party vigorously pushed ahead with industrial construction, and in the postwar period especially carried out this work on a large scale. In this way we have achieved great success in the creation of a modern industry.

The annual rate of growth of industrial production in the ten postwar years from 1954 to 1963 averaged 34.8 per cent. Our country's industrial output in 1964 was about 11 times that of the prewar year 1949 and more than 13 times that of the pre-Liberation year 1944.

As a result of the rapid growth of industrial production, the proportion of industry in the total value of industrial and agricultural output jumped from 28 per cent in 1946 to 75 per cent in 1964.

Heavy industry is the basis for the development of the national economy. Unless heavy industry is developed, light industry and agriculture cannot be developed, nor can all branches of the national economy be equipped with modern technique. Heavy industry is the material basis for the country's political and economic independence, without which we can neither talk about an independent national economy nor strengthen national defense capacities.

Our Party's line was to create our own basis of heavy industry equipped with new technique, relying mainly on domestic natural resources and raw materials for its development, and capable of meeting the demands of our national economy for materials, fuel, power, machinery and equipment principally with home products. This is the line of creating an independent, modern heavy industry.

It was of paramount importance in implementing this line of our Party to combine the rehabilitation, reconstruction and building of new heavy industrial plants in a rational way, correctly linking the development of heavy industry with that of light industry and agriculture.

What we had in the way of heavy industry was backward in technical equipment and was deformed and severely damaged. But, for all that, we could not abandon it. Our Party has followed the policy of rehabilitating the existing foundation of heavy industry, reconstructing and expanding it on the basis of new technique so as to make the most of it, while, at the same time, building such new industrial branches and enterprises as our country did not possess.

While steadfastly assuring the priority growth of heavy industry, our Party has also endeavored to build a heavy industry not for its own sake, but to build one capable of most effectively serving the development of light industry and agriculture and the improvement of the people's livelihood.

In this way we were able to build a powerful heavy industrial basis with comparatively small funds in a historically short space of time and, on this basis, rapidly develop light industry and agriculture also.

Our heavy industry has come to possess all key branches, is equipped with new technique and has its own solid raw material base. In 1964 our country's heavy industry produced 12,500 million kwh of electricity, 14.4 million tons of coal, 1.3 million tons of pig and granulated iron, 1.1 million tons of steel, more than 750,000 tons of chemical fertilizers, 2.6 million tons of cement, and large quantities of machinery and equipment and various other means of production.

One of our biggest achievements in the building of heavy industry is the creation of our own machine-building plants.

The revisionists, talking about "international division of labor," opposed our Party's line on the building of heavy industry and maintained, among other things, that our country did not need to develop the machine-building industry but would do well to produce only minerals and other raw materials. Of course, we could not agree with them.

Our Party started building underground machine factories already during the war, and has rapidly expanded the machine industry in the postwar period.

Entering the period of the Five-Year Plan, we set about developing our machine-building capacity on a large scale so as to produce by ourselves, as far as possible, not only medium and small machines and equipment and accessories but also heavy machines and equipment required by our national economy.

This was a very difficult task for us, as we had no experience and were lacking in technique. It goes without saying that those who did not approve of the development of machine-building in our country could not help us. When producing tractors, motor cars and other modern machinery and equipment for the first time, we had to do everything by ourselves, from designing to assembling. Our workers and technicians met with many a setback, but they strove with set teeth until at last they succeeded in turning out such machines and equipment, and came to mass-produce them. We also promoted a let-machine-tool-make-machine-tools movement on a mass scale to make machine tools in all places where there were machine tools, thereby rapidly extending the foundations of the industry and, at the same time, convincing our working people that they were capable of making machines of any type.

The machine-building industry of our country was created after such a tough struggle. But in the course of this our working people accumulated invaluable experience, gained a deeper faith in their own strength and talents, and came to take better care of the machines and equipment they themselves had made despite all sorts of difficulties.

Thus, though our country did not have a machine-building industry in the past, we are now producing mainly at home machinery and equipment, including generating, chemical and metallurgical equipment, motor cars, tractors, excavators and other heavy machines and equipment needed in our national economy. In 1964 the proportion of machine-building in industrial output was 25.8 per cent and the rate of self-sufficiency in machinery and equipment was 94.3 per cent.

Today our heavy industry, with machine-building as its backbone, constitutes the reliable material foundation for equipping all branches of the national economy with modern technique and for firmly guaranteeing the political and economic independence of the country.

Light industry was one of the most backward sections. We have made great efforts to build up our own basis of light industry capable of meeting the needs of the people.

Our Party's policy in the production of consumer goods for the people is to develop medium- and small-scale local industry side by side with large-scale central industry.

We have built many large-scale central industrial plants which constitute the backbone of light industry, and have constantly strengthened their technical equipment, thereby greatly increasing the production of various consumer goods.

But in view of the economic conditions of the country, we could not build many large-scale light industry factories at once. If we had relied on the large-scale light industry plants alone, we would not have been able rapidly to abolish the backwardness in light industry, nor would we have been able to meet the rapidly growing needs of the people in any way. A decisive measure was needed to bring about changes in the production of consumer goods for the people.

Our Party, therefore, decided to develop the production of consumer goods in an all-people movement, and put forward the policy of building more than one local-industry factory in each city or county. The working people in all parts of the country rose as one to implement the Party's policy and built more than 1,000 local factories in only a few months without spending much state funds, by mobilizing the idle materials and manpower available in the localities. This made possible the production of various consumer goods in large quantities. Our country now has more than 2,000 local-industry factories, the technical equipment of which has been strengthened considerably. Our local industry accounts for more than half the entire country's output of consumer goods.

Our experience shows that in view of the economic and technical peculiarities of light industry, it is, in general, rational to develop medium- and small-scale factories side by side with large ones. Especially effective in increasing consumer goods production and rapidly developing industry as a whole in the underdeveloped countries, is to build many local factories which are comparatively simple in technique and small in scale. The construction of local industry is also of very great importance to the even development of all the localities in the country, and especially to the bringing of industry closer to agriculture and the gradual elimination of the distinctions between town and country.

We have built our own basis of light industry, which consists of central industry and local industry, and thus have been able to assure our people's livelihood with consumer goods produced at home. Take the textile industry, for example. The output of fabrics increased 195 times over that before Liberation, with 25 meters of various fabrics per head of the population. The food industry and the production of daily necessities have also grown rapidly.

Our consumer goods are not yet of high enough quality and their variety is also not as great as is required. But our working people are proud that all the consumer goods they use are made by their own hands, and they use them with pleasure. In the near future we will solve the question of making the variety of consumer goods richer and raising their quality as a whole to the world level.

The rural question occupies a very important place in socialist construction.

The rural question involves the socio-economic position of the peasantry as an ally of the working class, as well as the development of the productive forces in agriculture, one of the two major branches of the national economy. The completion of socialist agricultural cooperativization marks a historic turning point in the solution of the rural question. But it still does not mean its final solution.

Following the establishment of the socialist system in the countryside, it becomes necessary, on the basis of steadily consolidating this system, to develop the productive forces in agriculture to a high level, create a bountiful life for the peasants, liquidate the backwardness of the countryside left over by the exploiter society, and gradually eliminate the distinctions between town and country. . . .

As the cooperativization of agriculture was nearing completion and as industry developed, our Party lost no time in setting into motion the technical revolution in the countryside.

The Party laid down irrigation, mechanization, electrification and chemicalization as the basic tasks of the technical revolution in the countryside, and started with irrigation.

Agriculture, unlike industry, depends largely on natural-geographical conditions, and climatic conditions in particular. Therefore irrigation is the basic guarantee of high and stable harvests in agriculture. We have in the postwar period conducted an all-people movement to remake nature on a large scale by irrigation, spending enormous state funds. As a result, we are in the main able to free agriculture from drought and flood, and have laid the solid foundation for production free from crop failure.

No little success has also been attained in mechanization, electrification and chemicalization. Our countryside now has 20,000 tractors (in terms of 15 h.p. units). This is equal to one tractor per 100 *jongbo* of crop area. And about 300 kilograms of chemical fertilizers are applied to each *jongbo*. In the pre-Liberation days our countryside had no electricity, but now electricity is supplied to 95.5 per cent of all the rural *ri* and 81 per cent of all the farm houses.

While energetically pushing forward irrigation, mechanization, electrification and chemicalization, we have exerted untiring efforts to introduce extensively the achievements of agricultural science and advanced farming techniques, and in particular to develop intensive methods of farming.

Thanks to all these measures agricultural production has continued to grow rapidly in our country. Grain output has doubled in comparison with the pre-Liberation period. Stock-breeding and other branches of the rural economy have also made great progress. The food problem, one of the most difficult problems in the history of our country, has been solved in the main and for some years now we have been self-sufficient in food supply.

As a result of the growth of the productive forces in agriculture and the vigorous advance of the cultural and ideological revolutions in the countryside, the appearance of our rural areas has changed, the livelihood of the peasants has improved, their political awakening and the level of their consciousness have been enhanced. Our socialist system of agricultural cooperative economy has been further consolidated and developed and a rational system of guidance and management of agriculture has also been established.

Needless to say, in view of the tremendous tasks of socialist rural construction the achievements in rural work are still initial ones. Nevertheless, we have laid a solid foundation for the construction of the socialist countryside. We have also found the right orientation for the solution of the socialist rural question through our own achievements and experiences, and we know clearly what we should do in the future in respect to rural work. Our Party and people will continue to solve the rural question competently on the basis of the achievements already made and in conformity with the orientation and tasks already fixed.

One of the most important questions in socialist construction in backward countries is the training of national cadres.

In the early years following Liberation we were very short of national cadres, technicians in particular, and this was one of the biggest obstacles in state administration and economic and cultural construction. The question of national cadres, therefore, was an acute problem for us.

The problem of the old intellectuals is of great importance in building up the ranks of national technical cadres. Whether or not old intellectuals are drawn into the construction of a new society greatly affects the economic and cultural development of the country and this is particularly the case during the early stage of revolution.

As a matter of course, the old intellectuals of our country come mostly from the propertied classes. They served the imperialists and exploiting classes in the past. However, as intellectuals of a colonial country, they were subjected to oppression and national discrimination by foreign imperialists and as a result they had a revolutionary spirit.

Taking into full account the important role played by the intellectuals in the construction of a new society and the characteristics of our intellectuals, our Party since the early days of Liberation has pursued the policy of accepting them and remolding them into intellectuals serving the working people. Inspired by the Party's policy, the majority of the old intellectuals came over to the side of the people after Liberation. They have taken an active part in the revolutionary struggle and in construction. Thus, they have made a valuable contribution, and continue to make one, to economic and cultural construction.

Through persistent education by the Party and the ordeals of the revolutionary struggle, especially the trials of the Fatherland Liberation War against the armed aggression of U.S. imperialism, our old intellectuals have now been transformed into excellent socialist intellectuals and have developed into important national cadres.

While remolding the old intellectuals, our Party has paid the greatest attention to training new national cadres from among the working people. With a view to rapidly expanding the ranks of national cadres, the Party adopted the policy of giving priority to the training of cadres and to educational work.

Though we lacked experience and all the necessary conditions, we set up no small number of institutions of higher learning, including a university, and expanded the educational network at all levels on a large scale immediately after Liberation. We continued to foster national cadres even during the grim war years, and after the war directed still greater efforts to the work.

Our country introduced compulsory primary education already in 1956 and enforced compulsory secondary education in 1958. We will enforce compulsory nine-year technical education in the coming few years.

Pupils and students comprising about one quarter of the total population are now studying in more than 9,000 schools at all levels in our country, college students alone numbering 156,000.

Another important policy consistently pursued by our Party in educational work and the training of cadres is the close combination of general and technical education, as well as education through productive labor.

We have reorganized the former secondary educational system to establish a technical educational system, and further improved the contents of education, so that all the younger generation may acquire a certain amount of technical knowledge along with general knowledge of the fundamentals of science. Our country has also set up a widespread study-while-work system of education—networks of evening schools and correspondence courses, factory and communist colleges. In them large numbers of working people receive secondary and higher technical education without being divorced from production.

Despite the country's hard economic conditions, we have thus directed enormous effort to the work of training cadres and to education, overcoming all difficulties and obstacles, in order to rid ourselves of backwardness quickly and accelerate the rate of advance. As a result, we have been able to build up the ranks of our own national cadres in a comparatively short time, and attained the possibility of raising even larger numbers of new cadres in the future. As of October 1964, the technicians and experts in all fields of the national economy of our country numbered more than 290,000. All factories and enterprises, including large modern plants, are operated and managed entirely by our own national technical cadres.

Thus, we have not only established an advanced socialist system in the northern half of the Republic, but have laid the economic and cultural foundations which enable us to manage the economic life of our country by our own efforts. This is a great asset for the happy life of our people and the future prosperity of our society. It also signifies that we have firmly built our revolutionary base politically, economically and culturally, a reliable guarantee for the unification of our fatherland and the final victory of the Korean revolution.

JUCHE AND THE MASS LINE

All our victories and successes in the socialist revolution and the building of socialism are attributable to the Marxist-Leninist leadership of our Party and to the heroic struggle of our people for the thorough implementation of the Party's line and policies.

What was most important for our Party in giving correct leadership to the Korean people in their revolutionary struggle and work of construction was to establish *Juche* firmly.

The establishment of *Juche* means holding fast to the principle of solving for oneself all the problems of the revolution and construction in conformity with the actual conditions at home, and mainly by one's own efforts. This is a realistic and creative position, opposing dogmatism and applying the universal truth of Marxism-Leninism and the experiences of the international revolutionary movement to one's country in conformity with its historical conditions and national pecularities. This is an independent stand, discarding dependence on others, displaying the spirit of self-reliance and solving one's own affairs on one's own responsibility under all circumstances.

The Korean Communists are making a revolution in Korea. The Korean revolution is the basic duty of the Korean Communists. It is obvious that one cannot make the Korean revolution if he is ignorant of or removed from the realities of Korea. Also, Marxism-Leninism can be a powerful weapon of our revolution only when it is linked with the realities of our country.

Masters of the Korean revolution are our Party and our people; the decisive factor in the victory of the Korean revolution is also our own strength. It is clear that one cannot make a revolution by relying on others, and that others cannot make the Korean revolution in our stead. International support and encouragement is also important in a revolution, but most important of all in advancing the revolution and bringing it to a victorious conclusion are the endeavors and struggles of ourselves, the masters.

In the world there are countries big or small and parties with long or short records of struggle. Nevertheless, all parties are fully independent and equal and, on this basis, cooperate closely with each other. Each party carries on its revolutionary struggle in the specific circumstances and conditions of its own country; by so doing it enriches the experience of the international revolutionary movement and contributes to the further development of this movement. The idea of *Juche* conforms to this principle of the communist movement, and stems directly from it.

The problem of establishing *Juche* has acquired special importance for the Korean Communists owing to the circumstances and conditions of our country and the complexity and difficulties of our revolution.

While resolutely fighting in defense of the purity of Marxism-Leninism against revisionism, our Party has made every effort to establish *Juche* in opposition to dogmatism and flunkeyism. *Juche* in ideology, independence in politics, self-reliance in the economy and self-defense in national defense—this is the stand our Party has consistently adhered to.

Our Party, holding fast to the principles of Marxism-Leninism, studies and analyzes the realities of Korea and, on this basis, determines its policies independently. We boldly carry out, unrestrained by any existing formulas or propositions, whatever conforms to the principles of Marxism-Leninism and the realities of our country.

We respect the experiences of other countries, but always take a critical attitude toward them. So, we accept experiences beneficial to us, but reject those which are unnecessary or harmful. When introducing the good experience of another country, we remodel and modify it to suit the actual conditions of our own.

Our Party has always maintained an independent stand in its approach to the international communist movement, especially in the struggle against modern revisionism. We are resolutely fighting against modern revisionism, and this fight is conducted invariably on the basis of our own judgment and conviction and in conformity with our actual conditions. We consider that only by keeping such a stand can we correctly wage the struggle against revisionism and make substantial contributions to the defense of the purity of Marxism-Leninism and the strengthening of the unity of the international communist movement.

If one fails to establish *Juche* in the ideological and political spheres, he will be unable to display any initiative because his faculty of independent thinking is paralyzed, and in the end he will even become unable to tell right from wrong and will blindly follow what others do. One who has lost his autonomy and independence in this way may fall into revisionism, dogmatism and every description of Right and "Left" opportunism, and may eventually bring the revolution and construction work to naught.

In our country, too, at one time there were some among the leading personnel who had been infected with dogmatism and flunkeyism. They did no small harm to our work. The dogmatists did not study our realities, and, disregarding them, sought to swallow undigested the experience of others and copy it mechanically. Persons of this sort, looking up only to others and accustomed only to imitating what they were doing, slid down in the end to a position of national nihilism, from which all that is their own is disparaged and everything foreign is praised. Such a tendency was most seriously revealed on the ideological front. The dogmatists, instead of studying, explaining and propagating our Party's policies, merely echoed other people like parrots. They even went to the length of denying our people's history of struggle and our revolutionary traditions. They attempted to paralyze the creative initiative of our scholars in scientific research, teach the students what they had copied from others in education too, and to discard all that is national and disseminate only foreign things in literature and the arts as well.

In our country the harmfulness of dogmatism was most strikingly revealed during wartime. It became all the more intolerable in the postwar period when the socialist revolution and the building of socialism proceeded apace. Moreover, in that period we came to realize gradually that the revisionist trend infiltrates through the medium of dogmatism.

In view of this, our Party in 1955 set forth the definite policy of establishing *Juche* and ever since then it has conducted a vigorous ideological struggle to carry it out. The year 1955 marked a turning point in our Party's consistent struggle against dogmatism. In fact, our struggle against modern revisionism that had emerged within the socialist camp began at that time. Our struggle against dogmatism was thus linked up with the struggle against modern revisionism.

It was most important in establishing *Juche* to strengthen the study of Marxism-Leninism among the cadres and Party members and, at the same time, to equip them firmly with the ideas of their own Party, its line and policies. We have energetically conducted ideological work among the cadres and Party members so that all of them may think in the way the Party would like them to, make a deep study of the Party's policies, work in accordance with these policies and strive devotedly for their implementation. Our experience shows that when the Party's ranks are firmly united ideologically and organizationally, dogmatism can be overcome, the infiltration of revisionism can be prevented and all work can be executed successfully in line with the Party's intentions.

At the same time, we sharply intensified among the entire Party membership and working people the study of our country's past and present, and our people's revolutionary and cultural traditions. We saw to it that in all sectors of the ideological front, including science, education, literature and the arts, the things of our own country are given priority, the national traditions are honored, fine national heritages are acknowledged and carried forward, and the advanced culture of other countries is assimilated too, not by swallowing it whole but after thorough digestion.

These measures have boosted greatly the national pride of our people and their spirit of independence, and led them to reject the tendency toward mechanically imitating things of others and to endeavor to do everything in conformity with actual conditions at home. As a result of the establishment of *Juche*, science and technology have been advanced with great rapidity, qualitative changes have taken place in education and in the work of training cadres, and a new, socialist national culture, congenial to the life and sentiments of our people, has bloomed and developed.

While establishing *Juche* in the ideological and political spheres, our Party in the economic sphere has held fast to the principle of self-reliance and the line of building an independent national economy.

Absence of the spirit of self-reliance leads one to loss of faith in one's own strength, to making little effort to mobilize domestic resources, and accordingly to failure to serve the revolutionary cause. We are carrying on the revolutionary struggle and construction work with a determination to make the Korean revolution by our own efforts and build socialism and communism in our country by our labor and with our domestic resources.

Needless to say, we fully recognize the importance of international support and encouragement, and consider foreign aid a necessity. But we reject the erroneous ideological point of view and attitude of slackening up one's own revolutionary struggle, merely hoping for a good international chance to offer itself, or making no effort oneself, merely turning to other countries for aid. Both in the revolutionary struggle and in construction, self-reliance should be given primary importance; support and encouragement from outside should be regarded as secondary. Only when one struggles in this spirit, can one expedite the revolution and construction in one's own country to the greatest possible degree and also contribute to the development of the international revolutionary movement.

During the period of postwar rehabilitation our country received from fraternal countries economic and technical aid amounting to some 500 million rubles (550 million dollars). This, of course, was of great help. But in those days, too, we put main emphasis on enlisting the efforts of our people and on using domestic resources to the full. At the same time, we endeavored to make effective use of the assistance given us by fraternal countries. In actual fact, it was our own efforts that played the decisive role in postwar rehabilitation and construction. There is no need to make further mention of our country's achievements in economic construction in the subsequent years.

We have thus, on the principle of self-reliance, laid the solid foundations of an independent national economy.

Economic independence is an indispensable requisite for the building of an independent state, rich, strong and enlightened. Without building an independent national economy, it is impossible to ensure the firm political independence of the country, develop its productive forces and improve the livelihood of its people.

Socialism means the complete abolition of national inequality along with class exploitation, and requires the all-round development of economy, science and technology. It is therefore natural that a socialist economy must be an independent economy, developed in a comprehensive way.

We by no means oppose economic cooperation between states or advocate building socialism in isolation. What we do reject is the big-power chauvinist tendency to restrain the independent and comprehensive development of the economy of other countries and, furthermore, to place their economy under one's own control on the pretext of "economic cooperation" and "international division of labor." We consider that cooperation should be based on the building of an independent national economy by each country, and that this alone makes possible the steady expansion and development of economic cooperation between states on the principles of complete equality and mutual benefit.

Today our country is developing its economy by relying mainly on its own technique, its domestic resources and the efforts of its own cadres and people; it is supplying the domestic needs for heavy and light industrial goods and agricultural produce mainly with its domestic products.

As for our country's economic relations with other countries, they are based on filling each other's needs and cooperating with each other on the principles of complete equality and mutual benefit. These relations find expression in foreign trade and in various other ways.

Having laid the solid foundations of an independent national economy, we have come to possess our own economic basis for increasing the wealth and power of the country and radically improving the people's livelihood. We have become able further to expand and develop economic cooperation with other countries. Our economic independence also constitutes the reliable material basis for guaranteeing the country's political independence and strengthening its defense capacities.

Along with the establishment of *Juche*, the thorough implementation of the mass line has been one of the most important questions in our Party's leadership in the revolution and in construction.

Considering that the decisive guarantee for the acceleration of the socialist revolution and the building of socialism consists in enlisting all the creative energies of the masses of the people and offering full scope for their enthusiasm, initiative and talents, our Party has held consistently to the revolutionary mass line in all its activities.

Our Party has been able to achieve tremendous successes in the socialist revolution and the building of socialism by relying on the high revolutionary zeal and inexhaustible creative power of our people who, grasping their destinies in their own hands, are determined to build a new life. Whenever it encountered difficulties and ordeals, the Party, placing faith in the masses of the people, consulted with them and enlisted their efforts and wisdom in overcoming these difficulties.

We have also carried out successfully many huge and difficult construction projects by unfolding a mass campaign. The let-machine-tool-make-machine-tools movement, the building of local industry, large-scale nature-remaking projects for irrigation, and the rehabilitation and construction of towns and villages which had been reduced to ashes—all these were carried out through mass campaigns, through all-people drives.

In our country, science and technology are also developing rapidly as a mass movement, through the creative cooperation of scientists and technicians on the one hand and workers and peasants on the other. Literature and the arts are also flowering with every passing day through the combination of the activities of professional writers and artists with the literary and art activities of the broad masses.

The method of relying on the masses and rousing them widely to activity is a revolutionary and positive one. It is a method that makes it possible to mobilize all the potentialities and possibilities to the full in the revolution and construction.

The Marxist-Leninist Party must at all times thoroughly implement the mass line, both before and after seizing power, both in the revolutionary struggle and in construction work. And the danger of weakening the mass line increases after the Party has seized power. Upon its founding after Liberation, our Party assumed the leadership of the government. Many of our functionaries had little experience in the revolutionary struggle and mass work in the past. For this reason it was particularly important for us to improve the method and style of work of the functionaries so as to implement the mass line.

Our Party has waged a vigorous ideological struggle to eliminate bureaucracy and establish the revolutionary mass viewpoint among the functionaries. The Party has made tireless efforts to get all the functionaries to acquire the revolutionary method of work, going deep among the masses, consulting with them, deriving strength and wisdom from them and mobilizing them to solve the tasks set before them.

The method of work, called the Chongsanri method* in our country, is an embodiment and development of our Party's mass line in conformity with the new realities of socialist construction. The essence of the Chongsanri method lies in the fact that the upper organs help the lower, superiors help their inferiors, priority is given to political work and the masses are roused to carry out the revolutionary tasks.

Through the popularization of the Chongsanri method, we have improved decisively the functionaries' method and style of work and brought about a big turn in the work of the Party, state and economic organs.

To give priority to political work is most important in bringing into full play the revolutionary zeal and creative energy of the masses of the people.

The Communists always fight in defense of the interests of the people and for their happiness. To this end, the broad masses must be awakened and mobilized. One of the inherent advantages of the socialist system is that the working people, freed from exploitation and oppression, display voluntary enthusiasm and creative initiative in their work for the state and society and for their own happiness.

To carry out political work well among the masses to induce them voluntarily to perform the revolutionary tasks is, therefore, an effective method, stemming from the character of the Communists and from the nature of the socialist system.

It is absolutely wrong to be immersed only in economic and

---

*Chongsanri derives its name from the *ri* of Chongsan, Kangso county in South Pyongan province, where Kim Il Sung in February 1960 first developed the proposal for a new system of economic management in the farm cooperatives, adapted to the merger of the cooperatives into *ri*-unit associations. (*see* Kim Byong Sik, *Modern Korea.*)

technical work while neglecting political work, to lay stress on material interest only, without raising the political and ideological consciousness of the working people.

Our Party has adhered firmly to the principle of giving priority to political work in all matters.

When we undertook any revolutionary task, we began by explaining thoroughly and bringing home to all Party members and the masses the Party's policy with regard to the task and saw that they held mass discussions about ways and means of executing the Party's policy, so that they would strive to carry it through with a high degree of political consciousness and enthusiasm. To enhance the class awakening and the level of political and ideological consciousness of the working people, we have also energetically carried out communist education among them in combination with education in the Party's policies and the revolutionary traditions.

Political work is none other than work with people, and it is basic to Party work. Apart from the Party's leadership, the masses cannot be mobilized, nor can socialism and communism be built. Only on the basis of enhancing the leading role of the Party and constantly strengthening Party work in all spheres, have we been able successfully to carry out the principle of giving priority to political work.

Thus, by energetically carrying on political work, work with people, which is the basis of Party work, we have been able to bring into full play the revolutionary enthusiasm and creative power of our working people and inspire them to mass heroism and to a mass labor upsurge.

The basic method our Party employs in mobilizing the masses in socialist construction is to raise the Party's leading role and invariably give priority to political work, combining this properly with economic and technical work, steadily to enhance the political awakening and the level of consciousness of the working people and properly to combine this with the material interest.

One of the very important problems in the carrying out of our Party's mass line was that of educating and remolding the masses of all strata and uniting them solidly around the Party.

The political unity and solidarity of the people in the northern half of the Republic is not only the decisive guarantee for building a new life there, but it also is one of the basic factors in unifying the fatherland and achieving the victory of the Korean revolution.

Our Party consistently and tirelessly has worked to rally the people of all walks of life closely around itself and turn our revolutionary base into a stronger political force.

The protracted colonial rule of Japanese imperialism, the partition of the country and, particularly, the sowing of discord among our people by the enemy during the war, have rendered the social and political composition of the population very complex. We, however, cannot make revolution with spotless people alone, rejecting all those whose social origin and whose records of social and political life are complicated.

Therefore, our Party, closely combining the class line and the mass line, has adopted the policy of winning over to the side of revolution all people, with the exception of the handful of malicious elements. Under the circumstances in which the socialist system had already triumphed, the Party's strength had grown decisively and the Party's authority and prestige had become unshakable among the masses, we considered that we were able to educate and remold all the people, except the conscious reactionaries of hostile class origin.

We boldly trusted and embraced even those whose social origin and whose records of social and political life were complex, and ensured them conditions for working in peace, provided they now supported our Party and displayed enthusiasm in their work.

Life has confirmed fully the correctness of this policy of our Party. By carrying out the policy we have been able, and are successfully continuing, to educate and remold the broad masses of people of various strata. Although the composition of our population is complex and we are standing tensely face to face with the enemy, our Party has today united the masses of the people solidly around itself, and a cheerful, exuberant atmosphere prevails in our society.

The all-people Chollima movement which has been unfolded

with untiring vigor is the most brilliant embodiment of the mass line of our Party.

The Chollima movement is a mass drive which organically links collective innovation in economic and cultural construction with the work of educating and remolding the working people. Through the Chollima movement all the wisdom, enthusiasm and creative energy of our people are brought into full play, innovations are effected in all spheres of economy, culture, ideology and morality, and the building of socialism in our country is greatly accelerated.

The Chollima movement is the general line of our Party in socialist construction. The essence of this line is to unite the entire working people more firmly around the Party by educating and remolding them with communist ideas, and to give full scope to their revolutionary zeal and creative talents so as to build socialism better and faster.

We will continue to develop the Chollima movement both in scale and in depth and thus expedite still more the building of socialism in the northern half of our country.

VI.

THE SOUTH KOREAN REVOLUTION

BEING A revolution for liberating one half of our country's territory and the two-thirds of its population still held in bondage by foreign imperialists, the revolution in South Korea is an important component part of the Korean revolution as a whole. For the unification of our fatherland and the victory of the Korean revolution, it is necessary to strengthen the revolutionary forces in South Korea while promoting socialist construction in the North.

Since the first days of their occupation of South Korea, the U.S. imperialists have pursued the policies of military aggression and colonial enslavement. As a result, South Korea has been turned entirely into a colony, a military base of U.S. imperialism.

The South Korean "government" is a puppet regime set up with the armed support of the U.S. imperialists: it is nothing but a tool faithfully executing the instructions of its U.S. overlords.

Through this puppet regime and with the use of so-called "aid" as a bait, the U.S. imperialists have placed all the political, economic, cultural and military affairs of South Korea under their control.

In the name of "joint defense" they have directly thrown their aggressive troops, nearly 60,000 strong, into South Korea. Moreover, in the guise of so-called "Commander of the U.N. Forces"

From Socialist Construction in the Democratic People's Republic of Korea and the South Korean revolution. Lecture at the Ali Archam Academy of Social Sciences of Indonesia, April 14, 1965.

the U.S. Army commander has absolute authority over the South Korean army.

Having occupied South Korea, the U.S. troops have barbarously assaulted and massacred innocent people in South Korea. They have introduced nuclear and rocket weapons, thus turning South Korea into their military base for aggression, and constantly jeopardized peace in Korea.

The U.S. imperialists' "aid" to South Korea is a major means of aggression and plunder.

They gave some $12 billion of "aid" to South Korea between 1945 and 1964, of this $3.6 billion was for economic "aid" and the remainder for military "aid."

The military "aid" goes to meet part of the military expenditure for the upkeep of the puppet army of South Korea, more than 600,000 strong. The South Korean army is a mercenary army serving entirely the U.S. policy of aggression. And the support of one division of South Korean puppet troops costs the U.S. imperialists only one twenty-fifth of the expenditure necessary for the maintenance of a U.S. army division. Thus, by conscripting the youth of South Korea for their aggressive purposes, the U.S. imperialists are saving large military expenditures while imposing heavy burdens on the South Korean people. Also by employing this huge puppet army in place of their own troops, they give the South Korean army an air of serving some sort of national interest.

The economic "aid" is also nothing but a means for subordinating the economy of South Korea to the ends of imperialist military aggression and colonial plunder. By incorporating "aid funds" into the budgetary system of the puppet government, the U.S. imperialists have obtained a tight grip on its budget and, through the allocation of these funds, control the banking organizations and enterprises in South Korea. In this way they control 45 to 50 per cent of South Korea's financial budget and 30 per cent of its banking funds, and monopolize 70 to 80 per cent of the supply of raw materials and 80 per cent of the imports. Today the South Korean economy is entirely dependent on the United

States; financial and economic organizations and enterprises in South Korea are in a situation where they will have to stop operations the moment U.S. "aid" is suspended.

All this demonstrates that U.S. imperialism is the real ruler in South Korea.

In order to secure a more favorable foothold for their colonial domination following occupation, the U.S. imperialists reorganized part of the socio-economic structure in South Korea.

In their aggression against South Korea, the U.S. imperialists attached prime importance to the fostering of the comprador capitalist, who was to play the role of middleman in the disposal of their surplus goods, act as fingerman for the infiltration of U.S. private capital, as agent in their plunder of the country's resources and as local purveyor of certain war materials.

They bolstered up the position of comprador capital by handing over to private capitalists and speculators, for a mere token payment, the properties formerly owned by Japanese imperialists, by enabling them to rake in exorbitant profits through their monopoly over the purchase and sale of the "aid " goods dumped by the United States in South Korea, or by other methods. The share of South Korea's comprador capital in key industries under the rule of the Japanese imperialists was barely six per cent, but today some 500 comprador capitalists have seized about 40 per cent of South Korea's manufacuring industry, around 80 per cent of its mining industry and more than 50 per cent of its foreign trade.

The U.S. imperialists have preserved the feudal system of exploitation in the South Korean countryside, which is favorable to their colonial domination and pillage. They imposed the so-called "agrarian reform," but this was only a piece of trickery designed to quell the demand for land by the South Korean peasants who had been inspired by the land reform in North Korea. Even after the enforcement of the "agrarian reform" the feudal relations of exploitation continue to hold sway in the South Korean villages and the peasant economy has become even more fragmented than before.

Today, about 100,000 landlords hold 40 per cent of the total arable land and exploit 1,400,000 peasant households in South Korea. The peasants have to pay land rent amounting to 50 to 60 per cent of their harvest, and most of them are shackled by debt to the landlords and rich peasants through usury.

U.S. imperialism has thus set up a system of colonial rule following its occupation of South Korea and, on this basis, has been enforcing an unprecedented military dictatorship over the South Korean people.

In South Korea, policemen and bureaucrats alone number more than 155,000. At present, 370,000 special political agents are rampant against the people.

This colonial-type social, political and economic system has become a weight which curbs the development of the economy and the democratization of social life.

Today the national economy of South Korea is totally bankrupt and its industrial output stands at no more than 85 per cent of that at the time of Liberation.

South Korea's agriculture is likewise in an acute crisis. Agricultural output has dropped to two-thirds of what it was at the time of Liberation. South Korea, once the granary of our country, has been turned into an area of chronic famine which now has to import 800,000 to 1,000,000 tons of cereals every year.

Today there are roughly seven million unemployed and semi-unemployed in South Korea. And each year more than one million peasant households suffer from lack of food during the lean spring months.

The national culture and the good manners and customs, peculiar to the Korean people, are trampled underfoot and the decadent and *fin-de-siècle* American way of life is corroding all that was sound in social life.

The people are entirely denied political rights and are exposed to terrorism and tyranny.

The economic catastrophe in South Korea and the wretched social position of its people have produced sharp social, class and national contradictions.

The basic contradiction in South Korean society at the present stage is that between U.S. imperialism and its accomplices—landlords, comprador capitalists and reactionary bureaucrats—on the one hand, and the workers, peasants, urban petty bourgeois and national capitalists on the other.

Therefore, to attain freedom and liberation, the South Korean people must drive out the U.S. imperialist forces of aggression and overthrow the landlords, comprador capitalists and reactionary bureaucrats who are in league with them. U.S. imperialism is target No. 1 of struggle for the South Korean people.

There can be neither freedom and liberation for the people in South Korea, nor progress in South Korean society, nor the unification of our fatherland, unless the U.S. imperialist aggressive troops are driven out and colonial rule is abolished.

Thus the revolution in South Korea is a national liberation revolution against the foreign imperialist forces of aggression, and a democratic revolution against the feudal forces.

The motive force of this revolution in South Korea is the working class and its most reliable ally—the peasantry—together with the students, intellectuals and petty bourgeois who are opposed to the imperialist and feudal forces. The national capitalists, too, may have a share in the anti-imperialist, anti-feudal struggle.

Our Party, with the support of the socialist forces of North Korea, has all along been waging a stubborn struggle to carry out the anti-imperialist, anti-feudal democratic revolution in South Korea by mobilizing all its patriotic, democratic forces.

The course of the South Korean revolution is beset with numerous difficulties and obstacles.

The occupation of South Korea by the forces of U.S. imperialism and its policy of aggression are the underlying factors of the complex, arduous and protracted nature of both the revolution in South Korea and the Korean revolution as a whole.

The U.S. imperialists need South Korea not merely as a market for their surplus goods or as a supply base of strategic resources. They also need South Korea as the military operational base for the occupation of the whole of Korea, as a bridgehead for attack on the Soviet Union and the Chinese People's Republic and aggression on the Asian continent, and, further, as an important strategic point for world domination.

That is why the U.S. imperialists have stationed in South Korea more than half of their Pacific ground force, although they are floundering in tight corners in all parts of the world today.

Thus, the revolution in South Korea has as its target of struggle a powerful enemy, the most ferocious and treacherous of all imperialists.

South Korea is the assembly ground and the den of the domestic reactionaries.

In contrast to what happened in North Korea, the remnant forces of Japanese imperialism were not liquidated in South Korea after Liberation. In order to establish a foothold for their colonial domination the U.S. imperialists actively protected and rallied the remnant forces of Japanese imperialism. The former pro-Japanese forces have now turned pro-American and have grown.

Moreover, as the revolutionary struggle was intensified in North Korea and the counter-revolutionary elements there sustained heavy blows, some landlords, comprador capitalists, pro-Japanese lackeys, traitors to the nation, vicious bureaucrats and fascist elements fled from the North to the South to join the reactionary forces.

In addition, not a few reactionary forces that had been scattered in foreign lands crawled back to South Korea.

The domestic reactionaries thus brought together, formed the counter-revolutionary core in collusion with outside forces, and turned against the revolutionary forces.

"Anti-communist" ideas are also deeply rooted in South Korea. For 36 years Japanese imperialism had malignantly infused "anti-communist" ideas, and after Liberation U.S. imperialism and its lackeys stepped up "anti-communist" propaganda, in a situation where the petty bourgeoisie made up the overwhelming majority of the population and the cultural level of the masses was very low.

During the Fatherland Liberation War the People's Army, when it advanced into South Korea, ideologically enlightened the people in the liberated areas to a certain extent, but the influence was not great because their stay in these areas was short.

As a result, a considerable proportion of the people in South Korea are still taken in by the "anti-communist" propaganda of the enemy. This is a serious obstacle to the development of the revolution there.

All this has created very difficult conditions for the revolution in South Korea, which has to go through many turns and twists.

This notwithstanding, the South Korean people have been waging a stubborn struggle, ever since Liberation, against the colonial fascist rule of U.S. imperialism and its lackeys, in defense of their right to live, for democracy and the unification of the fatherland.

Immediately after the August 15 Liberation the working-class movement surged forward rapidly in South Korea, and under its impact the struggle of the people in all walks of life mounted.

Inspired by the successes of the revolution in the North, the people in South Korea fought stubbornly against the U.S. imperialist policy of colonial enslavement, for the sovereignty and independence of their fatherland, and for democratic reforms of the kind that had been carried out in the North.

The general strike in September 1946 staged by the South Korean workers—who demanded food, higher wages, and an immediate halt to cruel suppression of every description by the U.S. military government and enforcement of a democratic labor law—developed into an all-people, anti-U.S. resistance in October, involving about 2,300,000 patriots.

In the years that followed, the anti-U.S., national salvation struggle of the people in South Korea—such as the February 7 (1948) national salvation struggle against the entry of the "UN Commission on Korea," which was rigged up by U.S. imperialism, and the struggle against the May 10 separate elections, so ruinous to the country, went on vigorously.

Struggles were waged by the soldiers of the puppet army, too. For example, in October 1948 there was a mutiny at Ryosu in protest against the barbarous suppression and slaughter of the people by the U.S. imperialists and their lackeys, in which even the local civilians joined. They smashed the puppet administration offices, and for a time they were in complete occupation of the city of Ryosu.

These struggles showed that the people in South Korea were resolutely opposed to the U.S. imperialist policy of colonial enslavement and the traitorous acts of the domestic reactionaries, and were firmly demanding the freedom and independence of the fatherland and the establishment of a democratic system. They demonstrated dramatically the revolutionary spirit and great strength of the masses of the people.

But the people's struggle in South Korea entered a period of temporary ebb owing to the setting up of a puppet, separate regime in South Korea in May 1948 and to the policy of fascization pursued thereafter by U.S. imperialism and the Syngman Rhee clique.

The U.S. imperialists and the Syngman Rhee cabal mobilized U.S. army units equipped with up-to-date arms to put down the mass movement, and perpetrated barbarous acts, arresting patriots at random, imprisoning and murdering them.

The U.S. imperialists also resorted to a crafty scheme designed to split and break up the revolutionary forces from within, by using the factionalists and spies who had sneaked into the leadership of the Workers Party of South Korea. As a result, at that time the Party organizations were totally destroyed and the revolutionary forces were split.

During the postwar years the people's struggle in South Korea embarked gradually upon the road leading to new advances.

Inspired by the successful socialist construction in the northern half, the people in South Korea in the postwar period have been fighting persistently against U.S. imperialism and its stooges and for democratic freedom and rights.

The massive Popular Uprising in April 1960, in which students and youth of South Korea played the central role, overthrew the puppet government of Syngman Rhee, the old minion of U.S.

imperialism. This was the initial victory of the South Korean people's struggle and dealt a heavy blow to U.S. colonial rule.

The collapse of the puppet Syngman Rhee government signified, in the first place, the bankruptcy of all its anti-popular policies and the notorious "march North" clamor.

In this heroic struggle the people demonstrated their revolutionary mettle, gained valuable experience, learned important lessons and were greatly enlightened politically.

After the April Popular Uprising, the situation in South Korea developed rapidly in favor of the revolution. The militant spirit of the masses, fighting against U.S. imperialism and its lackeys for the independent peaceful unification of the fatherland, ran high.

Thus, the struggle of the people in South Korea under the slogan, "Unification is the only way to life," began to develop into a movement for tearing down the barrier between the North and the South.

The U.S. imperialists, greatly alarmed by developments after the April Popular Uprising, engineered a military coup by aiding and abetting the fascist elements within the military, and subsequently stage-managed an insidious plot for the replacement of Chang Myon, who headed the second puppet government, with the Pak Jung Hi military fascist regime.

This, however, has only resulted in the further aggravation of the crisis in the U.S. imperialist machinery of colonial rule.

Last year witnessed another large-scale anti-imperialist, anti-fascist struggle of the students and youth in South Korea.

The struggle started in opposition to the reemergence of Japanese militarism and had as its purpose the shattering of the South Korea-Japan talks. Gradually it assumed an anti-"government" nature and developed into a struggle for toppling the Pak Jung Hi regime.

This patriotic, progressive struggle of the students and youth, which lasted over 70 days, from March 24 to June 5, dealt another heavy blow to the Pak Jung Hi clique and the U.S. imperialists.

While internally intensifying the policy of fascist repression and terror to crush the advance of the students, youth and the masses of the people today, externally the U.S. imperialists and the Pak Jung Hi regime are hastening to team up with the Japanese militarists. Furthermore, they are trying to establish an "anti-communist" Northeast Asia joint defense system.

None of these maneuvers, however, will enable the U.S. imperialists and Pak Jung Hi regime to cope with the ever-worsening crisis of their colonial rule, nor can they break the patriotic spirit of the people of South Korea who oppose U.S. imperialism and are striving to achieve the freedom and independence of their fatherland.

In South Korea today the conflict between democracy and reaction, between the patriotic revolutionary forces and the imperialist forces of aggression is growing more acute. The imperialist and reactionary forces are being isolated and weakened with each passing day.

The national and class awakening of the people is increasing gradually, their anti-U.S. sentiments are mounting and the trend toward independent peaceful unification is growing daily. The people in South Korea are being steeled constantly in the struggle, are accumulating rich political experience and becoming united in a more organized way.

At the present stage the basic line of the revolution in South Korea is to preserve the revolutionary forces from suppression by the enemy and, meanwhile, to accumulate constantly and strengthen these forces in preparation for the forthcoming great revolutionary events.

Most important in this connection is to firmly build a revolutionary Party and prepare the main force of the revolution in South Korea. To build the main force of the revolution means uniting around the Party the basic classes that can be mobilized for the revolution, namely, the workers and peasants.

In South Korea at present, the ranks of the revolutionary core armed with Marxism-Leninism are growing, the class consciousness of the workers and peasants is being heightened and their revolutionary strength is growing constantly.

It is important to form a united front embracing all social circles and strata on the basis of building a revolutionary Party and closely uniting the workers, peasants and all other working people.

The South Korean revolutionaries are directing special attention to combining the struggle of the workers and peasants with that of the youth, students and intellectuals. At the same time, they are endeavoring to form a broad anti-U.S., national salvation united front embracing all social circles and strata.

The growth and strengthening of the revolutionary forces and the formation and consolidation of the anti-U.S., national salvation united front can be realized successfully only under the condition of extensive mass struggle. Our Party supports actively, encourages and inspires all forms of the progressive, patriotic mass movements waged in South Korea.

In the final analysis, the revolution in South Korea can triumph only through the growth of the revolutionary forces of the people in South Korea and by their decisive struggle. Through struggle the people in South Korea further will be awakened and steeled and eventually will grow into an invincible revolutionary force. In this way, when the time comes they will surely drive out the U.S. imperialists and throw their lackeys overboard, thereby winning victory in the revolution.

The revolution in South Korea, no matter what method is employed, can be victorious only when the revolutionary forces are strengthened. Needless to say, once U.S. imperialism is driven out and the revolution triumphs in South Korea, the unification of our fatherland will be accomplished peacefully.

It is the duty of our Party to do everything in its power to expedite the growth of the revolutionary forces in South Korea and to assist the South Korean people in their revolutionary struggle.

It can be said that the unification of our fatherland and the countrywide victory of the Korean revolution depend, above all, on the preparation of three major forces.

First, further to strengthen our revolutionary base politically, economically and militarily by successfully building socialism in the northern half of the Republic;

Second, to strengthen the revolutionary forces in South Korea by politically awakening and closely uniting the people;

Third, to strengthen unity between the Korean people and international revolutionary forces.

Our Party is striving unremittingly to strengthen these three revolutionary forces.

It is of great importance for the victory of our revolution that the Korean people strengthen unity with the international revolutionary forces and isolate and weaken the U.S. imperialist aggressors internationally.

Our Party adheres steadfastly to the line of uniting firmly with the peoples of the socialist countries, and of actively supporting and strengthening unity with the peoples of the newly-independent nations fighting against imperialist aggression and the peoples of all countries in Asia, Africa and Latin America who are fighting to free themselves from the yoke of imperialism. We are endeavoring to strengthen solidarity with the progressive peoples of the whole world.

In this connection, it is of great importance to strengthen unity with the Asian, African and Latin American peoples and, in particular, to fight in unity with the entire Asian people to drive the U.S. imperialists out of Asia.

VII.

THE INTERNATIONAL SITUATION AND PROBLEMS OF THE WORLD COMMUNIST MOVEMENT

A FIERCE struggle is going on in the international arena today between socialism and imperialism, between the forces of revolution and of counter-revolution. The socialist forces and the national liberation, working class and democratic movements continue to grow on a worldwide scale.

The flames of the liberation struggle are fierce, particularly in Asia, Africa and Latin America. Imperialism is meeting with determined resistance by the peoples and is being dealt severe blows in these areas. The peoples who have risen in the struggle are winning fresh victories in their revolutionary cause of smashing the old world of imperialism and colonialism and creating a new world.

The growth of the revolutionary forces of the world headed by socialism and the collapse of the colonial system have weakened significantly the forces of imperialism. The internal contradictions of imperialism have become more acute and the discord among the imperialist powers has been aggravated. The imperialists are suffering telling blows from within and from without and are getting still deeper into hot water.

The revolutionary movement cannot be free from vicissitudes in the course of its development, but the general situation is

From *The Present Situation and the Tasks of Our Party.* Report at the Conference of the Workers party of Korea, October 5, 1966.

developing in favor of socialism and the revolutionary forces and to the disadvantage of imperialism and the reactionary forces. The victory of socialism and the downfall of imperialism are the main trend of our times that no force can check.

But imperialism does not recede from the arena of history of its own will. The aggressive nature of imperialism cannot change and imperialism still remains a dangerous force. The imperialists desperately try to find a way out of their doom in aggression and war.

The aggressive maneuvers of the imperialists led by the United States have become more open in recent years. The U.S. imperialists are perpetrating acts of aggression against the socialist countries and the independent national states, brutally suppressing the national liberation movements of the Asian, African and Latin American peoples and disturbing peace in all parts of the world.

Today, they direct the spearhead of aggression against Asia. They have brought more and more armed forces into South Vietnam in flagrant violation of the 1954 Geneva Agreements, carried out the scorched-earth operations of "burn all, kill all and destroy all," and have already extended their bombing of the Democratic Republic of Vietnam to the Hanoi and Haiphong areas. This shows that the U.S. imperialist policy of "escalation of war" in Vietnam has entered a new, serious phase. The U.S. imperialists are now running amuck to spread the war flames to vast areas of Asia.

The U.S. aggressors, occupying the southern half of our country, are making frenzied war preparations. They also occupy Taiwan, a territory of the People's Republic of China, and incessantly commit provocative acts against People's China.

The U.S. imperialists have revived Japanese militarism to use it as a "shock brigade" in their Asian aggression. They have aligned the forces of Japanese militarism with the South Korean puppets and are scheming to rig up a "Northeast Asia military alliance" with this alignment as the backbone.

The basic strategy of the U.S. imperialists in their Asian aggression is to blockade and attack the Asian socialist countries, stem the rapid growth of the revolutionary forces and prop up their colonial rule in Asia by concentrating more and more U.S. military force in this region, while mobilizing the forces of Japanese militarism and their satellite countries and puppets. This machination aggravates the situation in all parts of Asia to the extreme and gravely endangers universal peace.

The intensified aggressive maneuvers of the imperialists led by the U.S. are not signs of strength; they indicate, on the contrary, that the situation is more difficult for them. The desperate actions of U.S. imperialism in Asia, Africa and Latin America only testify that the forces of socialism are growing, the anti-imperialist revolutionary movement is unfolding intensively, and the imperialist foothold is shaken to its very foundations in these areas.

No amount of maneuvering on the part of the imperialists can check the mounting liberation struggle of the peoples or halt the triumphant onward march of socialism. The imperialists surely will be kicked out of Asia, Africa and Latin America and eventually defeated by the revolutionary struggle of the peoples. The ultimate triumph of socialism and the complete downfall of imperialism are inevitable. This is an inexorable law of historical development.

All events taking place in the international arena substantiate ever more clearly that U.S. imperialism is the main force of aggression and war, the international gendarme, the bulwark of modern colonialism and the most hateful enemy of the peoples of the whole world.

U.S. imperialism is target No. 1 in the struggle of the world peoples. It is the primary task of the socialist countries and the Communist and Workers parties to enlist and concentrate the broad anti-imperialist forces in the struggle against U.S. imperialism. Only by fighting resolutely against it can world peace be safeguarded and the revolutionary struggle of the peoples be crowned with victory.

In the present period the attitude toward U.S. imperialism is a major yardstick for verifying the position of the Communist and Workers parties. The Communists should always hold fast to the principled position of opposing imperialism, U.S. imperialism above all. Particularly today when it is expanding aggression in Vietnam, all socialist countries should take a still more frigid and tougher attitude toward U.S. imperialism. We should never tolerate renunciation of principle and compromise with U.S. imperialism in international affairs.

The socialist countries, even if they maintain diplomatic relations with the imperialist states, should not dissolve their anti-imperialist struggle therein or weaken it for that reason. The socialist countries should adhere to class principles in diplomacy, too, and should bring pressure to bear upon U.S. imperialism and expose and condemn its policy of aggression and war.

It is also wrong merely to shout against U.S. imperialism without taking concrete actions to stop its aggression. Particularly, one should not cause difficulties for the anti-imperialist forces taking practical and united measures against the U.S. imperialist aggressors. If this is done, U.S. imperialist aggression cannot be prevented. On the contrary, it will make the U.S. imperialists more arrogant and eventually encourage their acts of aggression.

It is a principle of the foreign policy of socialist countries to struggle against the imperialist policy of aggression and war, for world peace and security. While fighting to prevent war, however, the Communists should never fear it, but should annihilate the aggressors when they make armed attacks on us. Only by holding fast to the principled stand of opposing imperialism and by waging a resolute anti-imperialist struggle, is it possible to check imperialist aggression and defend peace.

Especially, the socialist countries should be duly vigilant over the fact that today the U.S. imperialists, while refraining as far as possible from worsening their relations with big countries, direct the spearhead of their aggression mainly against Vietnam and try to swallow up divided or small countries such as Korea, Cuba and East Germany, one by one. Attention should be directed at the same time to the possible maneuvers of the U.S. imperialists to ease the situation or maintain the status quo in Europe temporarily in order to concentrate their forces on aggression in Asia.

In this case, the easing of tension on one front by no means contributes to improving the general international climate, but on the contrary, provides conditions for the imperialists to intensify aggression on the other front. It, therefore, constitutes a greater danger to world peace and security.

In the present situation the U.S. imperialists should be dealt blows and their forces dispersed to the maximum in all parts of the world and on every front—in Asia and Europe, Africa and Latin America and in all countries, big and small. They should be bound hand and foot everywhere they set foot so that they may not act arbitrarily. Only in this way can we succeed in foiling the strategy of U.S. imperialism to destroy the international revolutionary forces, including the socialist countries, one by one, by concentrating their forces in this or that area or country.

Our Party and people will carry on an unflinching struggle against the forces of aggression led by U.S. imperialism and strive to unite with all forces opposing it.

To defend world peace, it is necessary to fight the allies of U.S. imperialism, while struggling against the main enemy. Struggles should be intensified against Japanese and West German militarism in particular.

Japanese and West German militarism have been revived rapidly under the active patronage of U.S. imperialism. They are being regenerated into hotbeds of war in Asia and Europe. Under these circumstances, the struggle against Japanese and West German militarism can never be neglected.

It is a good thing that the socialist countries are fighting against the militarism of West Germany. Our Party and people are opposed to the revival of West German militarism and its revanchist ambitions, and strongly denounce the U.S. imperialists for their criminal act of actively encouraging it. We support the struggle of the German people and the position of the German Democratic Republic against the rearmament of the West German militarists.

We must be aware of the danger of Japanese militarism in Asia along with that of West German militarism in Europe. As all the socialist countries struggle against West German militarism as well as U.S. imperialism in Europe, so they should fight against Japanese militarism as well as U.S. imperialism in Asia.

Japanese militarism has made its appearance in Asia as a dangerous force of aggression today. The Japanese militarist forces harbor the illusion of realizing their old dream of the "Greater East Asia Co-Prosperity Sphere" with the backing of U.S. imperialism. Japan's Sato government, with the active support of the United States, has not only mapped out plans of war to invade Korea and other Asian countries but already has started stretching out its tentacles of aggression to South Korea.

A tripartite military alliance virtually has been formed between the U.S., the Sato government of Japan and the South Korean puppet clique through bilateral military aggreements. The Sato government has become an active accomplice of U.S. imperialism in its aggression in Vietnam and is sending large quantities of war supplies, including various weapons, to South Vietnam to fill U.S. orders. Japan serves the U.S. imperialist war of aggression in Vietnam as a supply and repair base, as an offensive base.

At the instigation of the U.S. imperialists, the Sato government pursues a hostile policy toward our country and the other socialist countries in Asia. It also intensifies its economic and cultural infiltration into a number of Asian, African and Latin American countries under the specious name of "aid," "joint development" and "economic and technical cooperation."

The fight against Japanese militarism is a struggle to defend peace in Asia and the world and is an important part of the struggle against U.S. imperialism. All socialist countries should attach importance to the struggle against Japanese militarism and frustrate its aggressive designs by concerted action. Especially should they thoroughly lay bare and frustrate the attempts of Japan's Sato government to disorganize the anti-imperialist front under the guise of "friendship" for the Asian, African and Latin American peoples.

True, there exist certain contradictions between U.S. imperialism and Japanese ruling circles, and the socialist countries may take advantage of these contradictions in the interest of the anti-imperialist struggle when they are aggravated in the future. But we must view U.S.-Japanese relations in all their aspects. Despite their discord, U.S. and Japanese imperialisms are knit together in an alliance, subordinating the latter to the former, for their common interests in Asian aggression, and are in league with each other politically, economically and militarily. The contradictions between the United States and Japan should not be overestimated nor shoffld the subordinate position of Japan in the alliance be underestimated.

We should harbor no illusions as to the Japanese ruling circles and should pin no hope on them. If we overlook the danger of Japanese militarism and become intimate with the Sato government, it is, in fact, tantamount to encouraging the foreign expansion of the Japanese ruling circles and to consolidating the position of U.S. imperialism in Asia.

The socialist countries may develop economic relations with Japan but should not bargain with its ruling circles on political questions. The relationship with the Sato government should in all circumstances be formed in the interests of the Japanese people and of the anti-imperialist struggle as a whole.

Today the Japanese people are fighting against U.S. imperialism and Japanese monopoly capital in defense of the security of Japan and world peace. Their struggle deals a heavy blow at the Asian aggression of U.S. imperialism and Japanese militarism, and contributes to the cause of world peace.

The Korean people emphatically condemn the aggressive schemes of the Japanese militarists. The rearmament of Japanese militarism and its aggression against South Korea should be stopped decisively and the "South Korea-Japan treaty" concluded under the manipulation of the U.S. imperialists should be abrogated. Japan should free herself from U.S. imperialist domination and develop along the path of independence and democracy. The Korean people fully support and express militant solidarity with the Japanese people, headed by the Communist Party of Japan, in their struggle for the complete independence and democratic progress of Japan.

U.S. imperialist aggression in Vietnam and the struggle of the Vietnamese people against it are the focal point of the struggle between the forces of revolution and counter-revolution at the present moment.

The aggression of U.S. imperialism in Vietnam is not only directed against the people of Vietnam, but also against the socialist camp; it is a challenge to the national liberation movement and a menace to peace in Asia and the world.

The Vietnamese people have risen as one in the sacred battle, determined to smash U.S. imperialist aggression, liberate the South, defend the North, and unify the country. They are inflicting serious political and military defeats one after another upon the aggressors, thereby driving U.S. imperialism into a tight corner. The South Vietnam National Liberation Front has already liberated four-fifths of the territory and two-thirds of the total population, while the North Vietnamese people are repulsing successfully the barbarous bombings of U.S. imperialist air pirates. The heroic anti-U.S., national salvation struggle of the people of North and South Vietnam affords an example to the peoples of the whole world fighting against imperialism, for peace, democracy, national independence and socialism, and inspires them boundlessly.

On behalf of this Conference, I would like to extend the warmest militant greetings and congratulations to the fraternal people of North and South Vietnam who are attaining brilliant victories and accomplishing heroic feats in their righteous war of resistance against the U.S. imperialist aggresors.

The Vietnamese people are not only struggling valiantly for the complete liberation and independence of their fatherland but also are shedding their blood in battle to defend the socialist camp and safeguard peace in Asia and the world.

What attitude one takes to U.S. imperialist aggression in Vietnam and to the Vietnamese people's struggle against it, is a criterion that shows whether one is resolutely opposed to imperialism or not, and whether one actively supports the liberation struggle of the peoples or not. The attitude toward the Vietnam question is a touchstone that distinguishes the revolutionary stand from the opportunist stand, proletarian internationalism from national egoism.

All socialist countries and peace-loving peoples should oppose the aggression of U.S. imperialism in Vietnam and render every possible support to the people of Vietnam in their righteous war of liberation. As the Democratic Republic of Vietnam is subjected to aggression by the U.S. imperialists, the socialist countries should fight more sharply against them and make every effort to support the people of Vietnam. There should be neither vacillation nor any passivity whatever on this point.

All socialist countries should pool their strength and come to the aid of the fighting Vietnamese people and should foil the aggression of U.S. imperialism against Vietnam by joint efforts. At present, however, the countries of the socialist camp are not keeping step with each other in opposing U.S. imperialist aggression and aiding the Vietnamese people because of the differences among them. This hurts the fighting people of Vietnam and deeply grieves the Communists.

It is impermissible for fraternal parties to engage only in polemics over the Vietnam question at the present moment when the Democratic Republic of Vietnam is subjected to U.S. imperialist aggression. It is the Workers Party of Vietnam that is master of the Vietnam question. No one has the last say on this question except the Workers Party of Vietnam. As far as the Vietnam question is concerned, the fraternal parties should at all times follow the policy of the Workers Party of Vietnam and support its stand. As regards the aid given by fraternal countries to the Democratic Republic of Vietnam, too, it is none other than the Workers Party of Vietnam that can pass correct judgment on it, and the fraternal parties should respect it.

Today's situation is different from that of yesterday when the Soviet Union was making revolution all alone. Since there was no other socialist country in the world at that time, the Soviet Union had to cope with all matters, supply of arms included, by itself. But today, when there exists the powerful socialist camp, is there any reason why the Vietnamese people should not receive aid from all fraternal socialist countries in the harsh war against the common enemy? Socialist countries are duty bound to offer aid to the Democratic Republic of Vietnam, and the Vietnamese people are entitled to receive it. If the aid of socialist countries to the Vietnamese people is used effectively in the battle against the U.S. imperialist aggressors, then it is all to the good, by no means bad. In order to defeat the U.S. imperialists in Vietnam, all the brother countries should give more aid to the Democratic Republic of Vietnam.

Such, we consider, is the revolutionary stand of opposing U.S. imperialist aggression in Vietnam in deed and the internationalist stand of helping the Vietnamese people in real earnest.

Now is not the time for the socialist countries to stand by idly, only extending political support to the people of Vietnam. They should take more positive actions to aid the Vietnamese people. In the light of the situation in which the U.S. imperialists are expanding aggression against the Democratic Republic of Vietnam by bringing in troops of their satellite countries and puppets, every socialist country must dispatch volunteers to Vietnam to defend the southeastern outpost of the socialist camp and preserve peace in Asia and the world. This is the internationalist duty of the socialist countries to the fraternal people of Vietnam. No one is entitled to object to the socialist countries sending volunteers to Vietnam.

If all socialist countries assist the Vietnamese people in shattering U.S. imperialist aggression against them, U.S. imperialism will be doomed like the sun setting in the west and the revolutionary movements in all countries of Asia and the rest of the world will make great headway.

The Workers Party of Korea and the Korean people regard U.S. imperialist aggression against Vietnam as directed against themselves as well and regard the struggle of the Vietnamese people as their own. Our people will be more resolute in their struggle against the common enemy, U.S. imperialism, and will exert every possible effort to support the people of Vietnam. We are ready to send our volunteers to join the Vietnamese brothers in their battle whenever requested by the government of the Democratic Republic of Vietnam.

The sole and just solution to the Vietnam question lies in the four-point position of the government of the Democratic Republic of Vietnam and the five-point statement made by the South Vietnam National Liberation Front. The Workers Party of Korea and the government of our Republic extend full support to this just position of the Vietnamese people.

The U.S. imperialists are now staging a fraudulent "peace talks" farce in an attempt to cover up another plot of war escalation. No amount of deceptive artifice, however, can help U.S. imperialism cloak its foul aggressive nature. We strongly denounce their plot to expand the war of aggression in Vietnam and condemn their "peace talks" hoax.

The U.S. imperialists must desist from all acts of aggression against the people of Vietnam at once and must get out of South Vietnam without delay, taking their aggressive army, the troops of their satellites and puppets and all the lethal weapons with them. Should the U.S. imperialists continue to act recklessly in disregard of the repeated warnings of the Vietnamese people and the socialist countries and the strong condemnation of the peoples of the world, they will only suffer a still more ignominious defeat. Ultimate victory is on the side of the Vietnamese people who have risen in a righteous cause, and the U.S. imperialist aggressors certainly will be ruined.

One of the questions of international significance today is to defend the Cuban revolution. The victory of the Cuban revolution is the first socialist revolution won under the very nose of the United States; it is a continuation of the Great October Revolution in Latin America. It is a historic event that extended the socialist camp to the Western Hemisphere and marked a new turning point in the revolutionary movement in Latin America. The Republic of Cuba has become a base of revolution in Latin America.

Today, the Cuban people, under the leadership of the Communist Party of Cuba, are marching ahead unwaveringly in the front ranks of the anti-imperialist struggle, holding aloft the banner of revolution. The Cuban people are firmly safeguarding their revolutionary gains and building socialism in difficult conditions, valiantly repulsing the incessant acts of aggression and provocation perpetrated by the U.S. imperialists.

It is a sacred internationalist duty for the countries of the socialist camp and the Latin American peoples to defend the Cuban revolution. Socialist countries should give wholehearted support to the brotherly Cuban people in their revolutionary cause, safeguard the Cuban revolution and render positive assistance to socialist construction in Cuba. Communists who consider the interests of the revolution as the supreme law cannot act otherwise in relation to Cuba.

It is quite natural that Cuba should receive aid from socialist countries, and the fraternal parties and countries should be glad of it. This is demanded by the interests of the Cuban revolution and the revolution in Latin America. We should fully understand the circumstances in which Cuba is placed and the position of the Communist Party of Cuba.

The Communist Party of Cuba knows the Cuban question better than anyone else, and it alone can map out correct policies to suit the actual conditions of Cuba. All socialist countries are duty bound to respect the policies pursued by the Communist Party of Cuba and to support the struggle of the Cuban people. No attempt should be made to bring pressure to bear upon the Communist Party and people of Cuba and split the revolutionary forces in Latin America.

The Workers Party of Korea has given and is still giving full support to the just stand of the Communist Party of Cuba which, under the banner of revolution, correctly leads revolution and construction in its country and strives for the unity of the socialist camp and the cohesion of the international communist movement. Our Party and people resolutely condemn the aggressive moves of the U.S. imperialists against Cuba and powerfully support the heroic struggle of the Cuban people to defend their revolutionary gains and build socialism. We will continue to do all we can to cement our friendship and solidarity with the Communist Party and people of Cuba.

Tremendous revolutionary changes are taking place in the life of the Asian, African and Latin American peoples today. The national liberation movement of the Asian, African and Latin American peoples, along with the revolutionary struggle of the international working class for socialism, is a great revolutionary force of our times and a powerful factor in world peace.

It is amidst the unprecedented upsurge of the national liberation movement that so many countries have attained national independence and embarked upon the building of a new life. The peoples of those countries which are still under colonial oppression are fighting more vigorously for freedom and liberation.

But the imperialists, far from willing to get out of colonies meekly, are resorting to every artifice to seize and dominate even an inch more of land. They suppress the national liberation movement in Asia, Africa and Latin America and carry out subversive activities to tear newly-independent countries away from the anti-imperialist front one by one. While openly resorting to brutal force, they attempt to infiltrate into the newly-independent countries with "aid" as a bait, seeking to meddle in the internal affairs of these countries and disorganize them from within.

In recent years, the U.S. imperialists have intensified their subversive activities and plots against the newly-independent states. The U.S. imperialists bribe and rally the reactionaries, pitting them against the progressive forces, and seek to sway certain newly-independent countries to the Right. Their objective is to have those countries suppress the revolutionary forces internally, oppose the socialist countries, and disorganize the anti-imperialist forces externally.

India can be cited as an example. At imperialist instigation, the reactionary forces in India try to push the country farther to the Right. As the might of the socialist countries grows and the revolutionary movement develops in Asia, they fear their influence upon the hungry and ragged masses of the people. That is why the Indian reactionary forces aggravate relations with neighboring countries, while suppressing the progressive forces at home. By so doing, they are attempting to cover up the deepening social and class contradictions at home, diverting the attention of their people, and to prevent the revolutionary influence from coming in from without. We should be on guard against the reactionary forces of India who suppress the progressive forces at home while committing hostile acts against socialist countries.

Also, we cannot but direct our attention to the recent Indonesian situation. In Indonesia, the Communist Party and progressive public organizations have been outlawed by the Rightist reactionary forces, large numbers of Communists and progressive personalities have been arrested, imprisoned and slaughtered, and the anti-communist campaign is still going on. This is done at the instigation of U.S. imperialism as part of its plan for Asian aggression.

We condemn strongly the acts of suppression and massacre committed by the Rightist reactionary forces against the Indonesian Communist Party and democratic forces. We express firm solidarity with the Communists and progressive forces of Indonesia in their struggle against the machinations of U.S. imperialism and domestic reactionary forces to divert Indonesia to the Right, and for national independence and the democratic development of the country.

Developments in Indonesia offer a serious lesson to all Communists. They show that the more the revolutionary forces, including the Communist parties, grow, the more desperately foreign imperialism and domestic reactionary forces maneuver to stifle them. The Communists should maintain the sharpest vigilance and always be ready to counter possible savage repression by the enemy organizationally and ideologically, strategically and tactically.

The revolution is complex and requires the scientific art of leadership. A revolution can emerge victorious only when the line of struggle is laid down scientifically and scrupulously and only when the most appropriate time is chosen to unfold a decisive fight on the basis of a correct judgment of the revolutionary situation and an exact calculation of the balance of forces between the enemy and oneself. We should deeply bear in mind such experiences and lessons of the international revolutionary movement and make good use of them in our own revolutionary struggle.

Much is still to be done to abolish the imperialist colonial system in Asia, Africa and Latin America and achieve the complete liberation and independence of the peoples. The road of national liberation is a road of arduous struggle, in the course of which one encounters the desperate resistance of the imperialists and reactionaries and undergoes many hardships and trials.

The attainment of political independence is merely an initial step toward the ultimate victory of the national liberation revolution. Those peoples who have won independence are confronted with the task of opposing the subversive activities of foreign imperialists and domestic forces of reaction and carrying the cause of national liberation through to the end. For this purpose, the apparatus of imperialist colonial rule should be destroyed, imperialism and domestic reaction deprived of their economic footholds, the revolutionary forces strengthened, a progressive socio-political system established, and an independent national economy and national culture built. Only in this way, can the peoples of the newly-independent nations eliminate the centuries-old backwardness and penury left over by colonial rule, and construct rich and strong, independent and sovereign states.

The Workers Party of Korea and the government of the Republic actively support the peoples of all newly-independent countries in their struggle to consolidate national independence and bring about national prosperity. We shall continue to promote relations of friendship and cooperation with newly-independent nations.

Our Party and government consider it an important principle of foreign policy to support the struggle of the Asian, African and Latin American peoples against imperialism, for freedom and liberation. The Korean people sharply condemn the aggressive maneuvers of the U.S. imperialists against the Laotian people and fully support the struggle of the Laotian people for national independence. Our people support the righteous struggle of the Cambodian people against the aggression and intervention of U.S. imperialism and its stooges, for independence, neutrality and territorial integrity. We support the Asian, African and Latin American peoples, including the Congolese (K) and Venezuelan peoples, in their liberation struggles, and express militant solidarity with them.

We also support the working classes and the toiling peoples of the capitalist countries in their revolutionary struggle against the exploitation and oppression of capital and for democratic rights and socialism, and extend firm solidarity with them. Our Party and people will always stand firmly on the side of the peoples battling for peace and democracy, national independence and socialism, and will strive to strengthen solidarity with them.

The socialist camp and the international communist movement have been experiencing harsh trials in recent years. Modern revisionism and dogmatism have become grave obstacles to the development of the international revolutionary movement.

We can bring about the unity of the socialist camp and the cohesion of the international communist movement and fight on successfully against imperialism by overcoming Right and "Left" opportunism and defending the purity of Marxism-Leninism.

Marxism-Leninism has developed and attained victory in the struggle against Right and "Left" opportunism. As historical experience shows, various deviations from Marxism-Leninism emerge in the course of revolution. This is not so surprising. As long as imperialism remains and the class struggle goes on, this is reflected in the working class movement as Right and "Left" opportunism, and struggles are waged against them. This is somewhat inevitable.

Right and "Left" opportunism are bourgeois and petty-bourgeois ideas appearing in the working-class movement. They distort the revolutionary quintessence of Marxism-Leninism from both extremes and do harm to the revolution. We must fight against Right and "Left" opportunism on two fronts.

Modern revisionism distorts Marxism-Leninism and emasculates its revolutionary quintessence under the pretext of a "changed situation" and "creative development." It rejects the class struggle and dictatorship of the proletariat, preaches class collaboration, and gives up fighting imperialism. Besides, modern revisionism spreads illusions about imperialism and obstructs the revolutionary struggle of the peoples for social and national liberation in every way.

It is true that modern revisionism has already been dealt a severe blow by the principled struggle of the Marxist-Leninist parties, and is on the decline. This, however, does not mean that modern revisionism has been surmounted completely. Modern revisionism still remains a big danger to the international communist movement. It finds expression above all in the weak-kneed attitude toward imperialism and the passive approach to the revolutionary struggle of the peoples. We, therefore, cannot slight the struggle against modern revisionism.

We must fight "Left" opportunism as well as modern revisionism. "Left" opportunism takes no heed of the changed realities, recites individual propositions of Marxism-Leninism in a dogmatic manner, and leads people to extremist action under super-revolutionary slogans. It also divorces the Party from the masses, splits the revolutionary forces, and prevents a concentrated attack on the main enemy.

When "Left" opportunism is allowed to grow, it may also become as big a danger as modern revisionism, both to an individual party and to the international communist movement. Without fighting "Left" opportunism, it is impossible to unite the anti-imperialist forces to wage a successful struggle against imperialism, nor is it possible to battle effectively against modern revisionism.

Thus both modern revisionism and "Left" opportunism cause tremendous obstacles to the advancement of the international revolutionary movement. It is wrong to shut one's eyes to the danger of "Left" opportunism under pretense of opposing modern revisionism, and it is likewise wrong to ignore the danger of modern revisionism for reasons of fighting "Left" opportunism. Unless Right and "Left" opportunism are overcome, it is impossible to lead revolution and construction correctly in each country, nor is it possible to advance the international revolutionary movement vigorously.

The struggle against Right and "Left" opportunism is inseparably linked with the struggle for the unity of the socialist camp and the cohesion of the international communist movement. Our Party will fight on against Right and "Left" opportunism, and at the same time uphold the banner of solidarity. We should not commit the Leftist error of rejecting solidarity for the sake of fighting opportunism, nor should we commit the Rightist error of giving up the struggle against opportunism for the sake of defending solidarity. Our Party will do all it can to safeguard the unity of the socialist camp and the cohesion of the international communist movement, while carrying on an uncompromising struggle against Right and "Left" opportunism.

The socialist camp and the international communist movement are the deciding factor in the development of the history of mankind at the present time. They are the most powerful revolutionary forces of our times that are confronting imperialism and all the forces of reaction. The existence of the united and powerful socialist camp and international communist movement checks the imperialist policy of aggression and war and inspires the revolutionary struggle of the peoples of the whole world.

The imperialists are afraid of the socialist camp and the international communist movement more than anything else. It is for this reason that the imperialists have incessantly perpetrated and are perpetrating armed aggression and subversive activities against the socialist countries. The imperialists are now attempting to eat up the socialist countries one by one.

Under these circumstances, what is most important is to defend the socialist camp jointly from imperialist aggression and, for this purpose, the socialist camp must stand firmly united as one. And yet, the socialist camp fails to advance now in monolithic ranks, as a united force, due to its internal differences. This exerts a negative influence upon the development of the world revolutionary movement and the international situation.

It is a sacred duty of every Communist to fight to defend the socialist camp and uphold its unity. Communists must not tolerate any act that weakens the unity of the socialist camp. Renegades of the revolution must not be drawn into the socialist camp, nor must this or that country be excluded from it artificially. These are acts undermining the socialist camp. We cannot suffer anyone to destroy the socialist camp which was created by the working classes of the whole world with their blood. This is a matter of principle that concerns the destiny of the socialist camp and the future of the international revolutionary movement.

We cannot replace the socialist camp with any community of a different character.

To introduce the Tito clique of Yugoslavia into the ranks of the socialist camp and the international communist movement is to weaken the unity of the socialist camp and the cohesion of the international communist movement. The Tito clique of Yugoslavia betrayed Marxism-Leninism and broke away from the socialist camp and the international communist movement; they are opposed to the Declaration and Statement of the Meetings of Representatives of the Communist and Workers Parties* of all countries and have engaged in activities disrupting the international revolutionary movement. Such acts have long disqualified them from being admitted into the socialist camp and international communist movement.

*The reference is to the documents issued by the meeting of the Parties of 12 Socialist countries in 1957 and the meeting of 81 Communist and Workers parties in December 1960.

We have no objection, of course, to the socialist countries developing state relations with Yugoslavia. However, we cannot recognize Yugoslavia as a member of the socialist camp nor rank the League of Communists of Yugoslavia among the Communist and Workers parties. The wrong approach to Yugoslavia, together with other problems, constitutes an obstacle to restoring the unity of the socialist camp and the cohesion of the international communist movement today.

On the other hand, we should oppose the attempt to deny the existence of the socialist camp and to split the socialist camp and the international communist movement. The split of the socialist camp into two, the split of the international communist movement into two, and the split of each party into two cannot be a normal, and still less a welcome, thing. We must seek unity through struggle.

It is really regrettable for Communists throughout the world that differences among fraternal parties have gone so far beyond ideological and theoretical bounds today that they can hardly be settled. But, however serious they may be, differences among fraternal parties are still an internal affair of the socialist camp and the international communist movement. Differences among parties must not be developed into an organizational split, but must on all accounts be settled by means of ideological struggle guided by a desire for unity.

No socialist country must be excluded from the socialist camp and the international communist movement. No one should make an exaggerated or distorted appraisal of any fraternal country or party, or consider any of the 13 socialist countries as being outside the socialist camp and the international communist movement. We are of the opinion that utmost prudence should be used in appraising the leadership of a fraternal country or fraternal party.

Relationship between fraternal parties should in no way be identified with the hostile relations between us and imperialism. If the leadership of a fraternal party commits an error, the Communists should offer comradely criticism and help it to return to the right path.

Meanwhile, one should not form a hasty conclusion concerning the character of society in a fraternal country on the basis of isolated phenomena which may be observed in various aspects of its social life. The character of a given society is determined according to which class holds power and what form of ownership of the means of production it has.

We must grasp clearly the difference between the socialist and the capitalist countries. There exist fundamental contradictions between the socialist and the capitalist countries which originate from the nature of their social systems. These contradictions exist objectively, independently of one's subjective intentions. Various measures taken by the leaders may sharpen or alleviate contradictions between the socialist and the capitalist countries, but as far as the opposing social systems are concerned, the fundamental contradictions between socialism and capitalism can by no means be eliminated.

One should not put any fraternal country on a par with the enemy or push it away to the side of the imperialists, even if it has some negative aspects. The Communists can never allow themselves to be prejudiced or fall into subjectivism in their approach toward fraternal parties and countries.

Our Party considers it necessary to refrain from making a hasty judgment on fraternal parties or fraternal countries even if there are differences, and to take one's time to examine them through struggle. In the meantime, it would be possible to promote unity with them on the condition that they oppose imperialism, support the national liberation movement, and do not interfere in the internal affairs of other fraternal parties or countries. We must adopt a positive attitude of criticizing their negative side and helping them to rectify it, while appreciating and supporting their positive side.

In the opinion of our Party, it is a good thing that all socialist countries should continue to advance in the revolutionary ranks, proceeding from the interests of the international communist movement. Then, the might of the socialist camp can be strengthened and bigger blows can be dealt to imperialism.

The socialist camp is in a complex situation now because of the differences, but its existence is a hard fact. No one can liquidate the socialist camp at one's discretion. Even if anyone brings a non-socialist country into the socialist camp, it cannot become a socialist country. On the other hand, if anyone excludes a socialist country from the socialist camp artificially, it cannot cease to be a socialist country.

The socialist camp is an integral whole which is united on a common political and economic basis and knitted together by the same goal of socialist and communist construction. All socialist countries are in the socialist camp as equal members. The more countries are in the socialist camp, the better it will be. It cannot be a bad thing. The ultimate victory of the world revolution is achieved through the victory of revolution in each country and the expansion of the socialist camp.

Our Party has always defended the whole socialist camp and is opposed to all acts of splitting it. Our Party will continue to unite with all fraternal parties and fraternal countries, while fighting Right and "Left" opportunism. We will fight on determinedly to defend the unity of the socialist camp and the cohesion of the international communist movement based on the principles of Marxism-Leninism and proletarian internationalism, on the revolutionary principles of the Declaration and Statement of the meetings of representatives of the fraternal parties.

The U.S. imperialists now take advantage of the disunity of the socialist camp and the international communist movement to intensify aggression and plunder everywhere in the world. Particularly, U.S. imperialism is extending its aggressive war against the Vietnamese people by mobilizing a huge number of troops.

It is true that the peace-loving peoples on all the continents of Asia, Africa, Latin America, Europe, etc., are now waging extensive campaigns to oppose U.S. imperialist aggression and support the heroic struggle of the Vietnamese people. But the Communists cannot be satisfied with this alone. We must better organize the struggle to aid the Vietnamese people against the aggressive war of U.S. imperialism on a worldwide scale and advance it to a higher stage. As the U.S. imperialists are

THE INTERNATIONAL SITUATION

escalating the war of aggression in Vietnam, so the peoples of the world should escalate their struggle to oppose U.S. imperialism and aid the Vietnamese people.

To this end, it is most important to achieve anti-imperialist joint action on an international scale and form an anti-imperialist united front.

The attainment of anti-imperialist joint action and an anti-imperialist united front is the most acute question of principle in the international communist movement today. It concerns the fundamental questions of whether the U.S. imperialist policy of aggression and war can be checked or not, whether the socialist camp can be defended or not, whether the national liberation movement can be stepped up or not and whether world peace and security can be safeguarded or not.

Anti-imperialist joint action and the anti-imperialist united front, when realized, will make it possible to unfold the campaign to aid the Vietnamese people more powerfully, to frustrate the U.S. imperialists' policy of aggression and war, and safeguard Asian and world peace. It can also provide conditions for gradually overcoming the differences among the fraternal parties and recovering the unity of the socialist camp and the cohesion of the international communist movement, and will make it possible to accelerate more effectively the revolutionary movement in all countries. Anti-imperialist joint action is, therefore, absolutely necessary for the benefit not only of the cause of peace but of the cause of revolution.

As soon as U.S. imperialism started armed aggression against Vietnam, our Party proposed to wage an anti-imperialist joint struggle to make a collective counterattack on the aggressors. A number of other fraternal parties have proposed the same.

But the anti-imperialist joint struggle has not been realized due to the differences within the international communist movement. We consider that the socialist countries and the Communist and Workers parties must tide over this situation and pool their strength in opposing U.S. imperialism and aiding the people of Vietnam in their struggle.

All socialist countries have, on a number of occasions, condemned the Vietnam aggression by U.S. imperialism and expressed the positions of their parties and states in support of the fighting Vietnamese brothers. And all of them are giving economic and military aid to the people of Vietnam. The Communist and Workers parties in the capitalist countries, too, are active in their struggle to oppose the U.S. imperialist war of aggression and support the Vietnamese people.

We, therefore, consider that despite differences over a number of questions, there is an initial basis for taking anti-imperialist joint action, first of all, in countering U.S. imperialist aggression against Vietnam and aiding the Vietnamese people. We should not ignore this and should strive actively to form an anti-imperialist united front.

Refusal to take joint action against imperialism is not an attitude of truly opposing revisionism and defending the purity of Marxism-Leninism, or of contributing to the strengthening of the unity of the socialist camp and the cohesion of the international communist movement, and cannot be regarded as a stand of opposing U.S. imperialism and aiding the fighting Vietnamese people.

The basic strategy of the world revolution today is to direct the spearhead of attack at U.S. imperialism. We must clearly distinguish a friend who has made an error from a foe. The foe should be beaten, whereas the friend who has made a mistake should be criticized and guided to take the right path. We should in this way join efforts with all friends and fight the main enemy.

In the struggle against U.S. imperialism, we must strive to take joint action with the Communist and Workers parties and democratic public organizations of all countries and with international democratic organizations. It is true that these organizations are not of the same opinion on various problems; their positions, too, differ from each other and their composition is also complex. But they have the vast masses behind them. To enlist still larger masses in the anti-imperialist struggle, the Communists must not reject joint action with these organizations.

Communists should not get stuck on differences but turn their attention to common points in their views, should always see matters in all their aspects, and refrain from going to extremes. If we fail to take joint action with the Communist and Workers parties and democratic public organizations of all countries and international democratic organizations, the vast masses united under them will fall away from the anti-imperialist front. Without the masses there is no carrying on the revolution. By taking joint action with these organizations, we can approach and exert revolutionary influence upon the masses under them, and mobilize them for the anti-imperialist struggle. To refuse to take anti-imperialist joint action means divorcing oneself from the masses and going in for isolationism; in fact, it will only bring about the serious consequence of undermining the anti-imperialist struggle.

Communists should under no circumstances be hidebound. We must rally all the anti-imperialist forces and unfold a struggle against imperialism by a united force. It is a basic principle of the communist strategy and tactics today to extend the anti-imperialist front by winning over more allies, even if they are not a consistent and steadfast force, to isolate U.S. imperialism to the greatest possible extent and deal it blows by joint action.

The history of the international communist movement knows many instances of the Communists taking joint action with the right-wing Social-Democrats in the struggle against imperialist wars. The united front policy of the Communists played an important role in the past in mobilizing the people for struggle against imperialist wars.

In the historical conditions of today when the world's socialist forces have grown stronger, there exist greater possibilities for realizing anti-imperialist joint action on an international scale. Drawing on the historical experience of the international communist movement, we must exploit even the slightest possibility to unfold a powerful anti-imperialist joint struggle.

It has become an international trend today to condemn the aggressive war of U.S. imperialism in Vietnam and give support to the Vietnamese people. Even those who once took to revisionism have found it hardly possible to hold out before world public opinion without supporting the Vietnamese people. This is a good thing and by no means bad.

Of course, there can be various categories of people among those who come out against U.S. imperialism in support of the Vietnamese people. There may be some who condemn the U.S. imperialists' aggression and support the Vietnamese people in order to make up for their past mistakes which they repent. Others may join in the anti-imperialist struggle, though reluctantly, under pressure from their own people and the peoples throughout the world, although their fundamental position still remains unchanged.

But, whatever their motives, it is necessary to enlist all these forces in the anti-imperialist joint struggle. If there is one who would like to rectify his past mistakes, at least in the Vietnam question, this is undoubtedly a good, welcome thing. And even if one opposes U.S. imperialism and supports the Vietnamese people, though reluctantly under pressure from the peoples, that will likewise be conducive, and not inimical, to the anti-imperialist struggle.

It is our belief that the more forces are drawn into the anti-imperialist joint struggle, the better it will be. It is necessary to induce those who shun the anti-imperialist struggle to join the struggle and encourage those who are passive to become active.

Furthermore, the joint struggle against U.S. imperialism will draw a clear line of demarcation between the Marxist-Leninists and the revisionists. It will be clarified through actual struggle whether one's opposition to U.S. imperialism or whether one's support to the Vietnamese people is real or sham. Practice is the yardstick that tells right from wrong. Opportunism also can be overcome in the practical revolutionary struggle as well as in the ideological struggle.

In realizing joint action, Communists must always adhere to the principle of uniting while struggling and of struggling while uniting. The joint action we advocate does not mean unconditional unity or unprincipled compromise. What we mean is to take concerted action and join efforts with the anti-imperialist forces in opposing U.S. imperialism and supporting the Vietnamese people, while abiding by Marxist-Leninist principles. In this way we should, in the course of our joint struggle, criticize and overcome the opportunist elements, support and encourage the anti-imperialist aspects.

We consider that anti-imperialist joint action by no means conflicts with the struggle against revisionism. Rather, it is a positive form of struggle against opportunism of all hues. It is a correct policy to realize joint action and a united front against imperialism, a policy which makes it possible not only to carry on a successful struggle against imperialism but to bring about the revolutionary awakening of the masses of the people, oppose all kinds of opportunism, and safeguard the purity of Marxism-Leninism.

It is an urgent task for the Communists of the whole world today to work out and take concrete measures for joint action in opposing U.S. imperialism and supporting the Vietnamese people.

We deem it necessary for the socialist countries, first of all, to dispatch international volunteers to assist the fighting people of Vietnam. This will be the first step toward the realization of joint action against imperialism. If we dispatch international volunteers to Vietnam, it will prove a powerful blow at the U.S. imperialist aggressors and make them desist from reckless escalation of the war of aggression in Vietnam.

We should actively endeavor to see that the international democratic organizations also take anti-imperialist joint action. These organizations must make it their central task in their activities to oppose U.S. imperialism and give support to the fighting peoples. Thus, the democratic public organization in all countries should be made to achieve anti-imperialist joint action through the medium of the international democratic organizations, and all the international democratic organizations should take joint action to oppose U.S. imperialism and support the peoples of the fighting countries in union. If anti-imperialist joint action is achieved in this way in the activities of the international democratic organizations, it will be a great force.

But these measures alone will not solve fully the question of realizing anti-imperialist joint action and united front. The most important thing is to provide conditions for the fraternal parties to attain anti-imperialist joint action. The Communist and Workers parties should, first of all, wage an uncompromising struggle against imperialism and give active support to the revolutionary movements of the peoples, each from its own position. On this course, we should gradually narrow down the differences and create an atmosphere conductive to mutual contacts. And when definite conditions are created, the fraternal parties may hold a consultation and discuss the question of anti-imperialist joint action in a concrete way.

To work actively in this way to realize anti-imperialist joint action and anti-imperialist united front on an international scale by overcoming all difficulties, we believe, is the way for all the fraternal parties to be loyal to Marxist-Leninist principles and discharge their internationalist duties at the present time.

It is a matter of importance in the international communist movement that the Communist and Workers parties maintain independence. Only when each party has independence can it carry on successfully the revolution in its country and contribute to the world revolution, and can the cohesion of the international communist movement be strengthened.

To be independent is each party's sacred right which no one is allowed to violate, and each party is duty bound to respect the independence of other fraternal parties. Respect for independence is a prerequisite for and basic to the unity and cooperation of the fraternal parties. This unity and cooperation can be truly voluntary, solid and comradely only if all of them respect each other's independence.

The mutual relations of fraternal parties should be based on the principles of complete equality, independence, mutual respect, non-interference in each other's internal affairs, and comradely cooperation. These norms were defined at the 1957 and 1960 meetings of representatives of the parties of all countries on the basis of the historical experience of the international communist movement, and their correctness has already been confirmed in life. The Communist and Workers parties without exception must strictly observe these norms and be true to them. If they are ever violated, complicated problems arise between the fraternal parties, the unity of the international communist movement is marred, and many difficulties crop up in the forward movement.

In recent years there have been incessant violations of the norms governing the mutual relations of the fraternal parties in the international communist movement. This has given rise to complicated problems in the international communist movement and created serious obstacles to the unity of fraternal parties.

All parties must respect other parties on an equal footing and strive to maintain comradely relations with each other. There can be neither a senior nor a junior party, nor a party that leads and party that is led among the Communist and Workers parties. No party is entitled to claim a privileged position in the international communist movement.

In the international communist movement there is no international organization which exercises unified leadership over the activities of the parties of all countries. The times have changed and the days are gone when the communist movement needed an international center. After the dissolution of the Third International there is no "center" or "pivot" in the international communist movement. It is therefore impossible that a "pivot" of the revolution should shift from one country to another. It is impossible, moreover, that a certain country becomes the "pivot of the world revolution" or a certain party becomes the "leading party" in the international communist movement.

The revolution in each country is carried out by its own people under the leadership of its own party, and not by a certain international "center" or by the party of any other country. Communists accept no "pivot" or "center" whatsoever in the international communist movement. If they accepted it, it would mean that a certain party is allowed to enjoy a privileged position. Then that party would rise to a higher position from where it would be able to give instructions and orders to other parties, while the latter would be compelled to obey and worship the former. Should such a relationship be allowed to exist between the fraternal parties, it will deprive each party of its independence and even prevent it from carrying on the revolution and construction in its own country independently. This kind of relationship can never be tolerated in the international communist movement.

The Communist and Workers parties, all as equal members of the international communist movement, are making contributions jointly to the development of the international revolutionary movement and Marxism-Leninism.

If they are to play the role of the advanced detachment in the revolution, the Communist and Workers parties must be guided only by Marxism-Leninism. Marxism-Leninism is the most scientific and revolutionary theory tested in practice and the acme of all the progressive ideologies of mankind. It sets out general laws which must be observed without fail in the revolution and construction in all countries.

Each party, applying Marxism-Leninism creatively to the realities of its country, should work out and carry into practice its own guiding theory for the revolution and construction in its own country. It cannot lead the revolution and construction with the guiding theory of other parties.

Each party's guiding theory has significance only within the bounds of its country. Each country's realities being different from the others', the guiding theory of its party, however excellent, does not fit another country. It is therefore impossible to present the guiding theory of the party of a certain country as one for Communists of all lands to follow, and it must not be imposed upon other parties.

For the Korean Communists the only guiding principle is Marxism-Leninism and the lines and policies of our Party worked out through its creative application to the actual conditions of our country. For us there can be no other guiding ideology than this.

The Communists must under no circumstances be presumptuous or impose their views upon other parties. It is impermissible among Communist and Workers parties that a party should bring pressure to bear upon the parties of other countries or interfere in their internal affairs because the latter do not toe its line. In the international communist movement, however, there still are instances of some parties imposing their views and line upon other parties and bringing pressure to bear upon the latter, interfering in their internal affairs because they do not accept those views.

Interference by certain fraternal parties in the internal affairs of the Communist Party of Japan is one such instance. Even if there exist differences, fraternal parties should not support the anti-party factionalists within another party, sow confusion in it and split the democratic movement in its country. Interference from outside has brought great difficulties to the activities of the Communist Party of Japan. Because of these difficulties, the Communist Party of Japan opposes interference in its internal affairs, upholds its independence consistently, and, unwavering, is leading the revolutionary struggle of the Japanese people.

Our Party, too, has had a bitter experience of interference by great-power chauvinists in its internal affairs. Needless to say, those great-power chauvinists met with rebuffs. At that time, in the interests of the revolution and proceeding from a desire to preserve unity, we settled the issue in confidence, though it was hard for us to endure. In the future, too, we should oppose all manner of interference in our internal affairs and guard against great-power chauvinism.

In the international communist movement no party has a monopoly of the right to impose arbitrary conclusions on problems of principle. No party should assert arbitrary conclusions on important international issues and force other parties to accept them. Communist and Workers parties must discuss matters of common concern and act in line with the conclusions agreed upon between them. Only then can the unity of purpose and action be guaranteed.

Each party should be careful not to fall into subjectivism in dealing with important international issues or in its relations to fraternal parties. Communists must not appraise any fraternal party hastily or harbor prejudices against it because the latter is not obedient to them or has different views. No party must regard other fraternal parties as going against Marxism-Leninism because their positions are different from its own. And let there be no such practices as arbitrarily attaching various labels to the fraternal parties which maintain an independent position.

There are certain persons at present who attach the labels of "centrism," " eclecticism," "opportunism," and the like to our Party and other Marxist-Leninist parties. They say we are taking the "road of unprincipled compromise" and "straddling two chairs." This is nonsense. We have our own chair. Why should we throw away our own chair and sit uncomfortably straddling two chairs belonging to others? We will always sit on our steady Marxist-Leninist chair. Those who accuse us of straddling two chairs when we are sitting on our own steady chair, are themselves no doubt sitting on a chair crooked to the left or to the right.

The slanders against our Party merely serve to prove that our Party not only opposes Right opportunism but also is uncompromising with "Left" opportunism, and firmly adheres only to the principled stand of Marxism-Leninism. We oppose opportunism of all hues because we are Marxist-Leninists.

A Communist should not argue haughtily that whatever he does is right and whatever others do is wrong. It is impermissible to behave like this among comrades fighting for the common cause. Communists may have different opinions on this or that matter, though they are all guided by Marxism-Leninism. But even in such cases, they must have an understanding of each other, hold sincere consultations and strive for unity. This is the rule of conduct the Communists must observe.

All Communists have their own standpoint and can tell right from wrong. Just because a party has ties with other parties, it cannot be regarded unjustly as subscribing to the latter's line and policies or blindly taking the cue from them. Regarding others with suspicion is a specific feature of great-power chauvinism and factionalism. Great-power chauvinists and factionalists suspect others for no reason and like to separate people into "sides." We will not take any "side." If someone asks us which "side" we are on, we will answer we are on the "side" of Marxism-Leninism, on the "side" of the revolution. Communists should not look at the independent activities of fraternal parties through tinted glasses and should not be too nervous about them.

The activities of all Communist and Workers parties cannot be fitted into any set pattern. The policies of fraternal parties cannot be the same, because the actual conditions and revolutionary tasks in each country are different from those in other countries. The unified line of the international communist movement by no means excludes diversity in the policies of individual parties.

Communists must curb great-power chauvinism in the international communist movement. This requires that no fraternal party should follow anyone implicitly, but each party should have independence and reject great-power chauvinism. All parties should unite and prevent anyone from holding sway over the socialist camp and the international communist movement, and preclude great-power chauvinism from exerting influence. If no one echoes and follows great-power chauvinism, no matter who may display it, it will become impotent and produce no effect. Only when great-power chauvinism disappears, can the independence of all parties be firmly assured and the relations between fraternal parties developed in a healthy way.

Communists must learn to hold fast to their conviction under whatever circumstances. A Communist, if he really is one, cannot follow in the wake of others blindly, parroting what they say and moving about in others' footsteps without following his own conviction.

It is not on instructions from anyone nor to curry favor that Communists are engaged in the revolution. Communists carry on the revolution out of their own faith in Marxism-Leninism for the emancipation of the working class and the working people in their own countries, for the great cause of the international working class. It is a noble trait of Communists to adhere to their conviction and fight unyieldingly for it.

The present situation in the international communist movement obliges us to maintain independence and autonomy more firmly. If we lack independence and autonomy and follow in others' footsteps in present-day conditions, we cannot have principle and consistency in our line and policies. This not only will eventually cause enormous harm to our revolution and construction, but will inflict a great loss on the international communist movement.

We cannot, and will never, dance to the tune of others. Proceeding from Marxist-Leninist principles and the actual conditions of our country, we should work out our line and policies for ourselves and implement them. In this way, we should push ahead vigorously with the revolution and construction. In the sphere of international activities, too, we must uphold our independent position in accordance with our conviction.

Our Party's independent position is linked closely with the principle of proletarian internationalism. Being internationalists, we categorically reject isolationism and nationalism. We treasure immensely the international solidarity of the working class and value unity and cooperation with fraternal parties and countries. We deem it necessary to respect the experience of other parties and learn from each other. What we are against is the tendency to follow others blindly without independence, depend wholly on others without faith in one's own strength, swallow the experience of others in one gulp without digesting it critically.

We should develop continually our relations with fraternal parties and fraternal countries on the basis of a correct combination of the principles of independence and unity. We maintain that the socialist camp and the international communist movement should unite in accordance with the principles of Marxism-Leninism and proletarian internationalism, in accordance with the Declaration and Statement of the meetings of representatives of the fraternal parties.

To unite and cooperate on the basis of equality and independence and to maintain independence while consolidating international solidarity is the firm and steady policy consistently followed by our Party in its relations with fraternal parties and countries. This policy not only accords with the interests of the revolution and construction in our country but fully conforms to the interests of the international communist movement. It is conducive to surmounting the difficulties existing in the international communist movement at present and achieving genuine unity.

World developments and the events in the international communist movement in recent years have once again clearly testified to the correctness of the line and policies of our Party.

All our successes are associated with our Party's line of independence. It is thanks to this line that our Party has not made Right or "Left" deviations in its internal and external activities and has been able to avoid errors on matters of principle.

Today the international prestige of our Party has grown and the international position of our Republic has been consolidated. We have won innumerable friends and sympathizers throughout the world. Our Party's line of independence in the international communist movement is receiving support from more and more fraternal parties. The achievements scored by our Party in its foreign activities inspire us with due confidence and pride.

Our Party will, as in the past, continue to hold fast to the line of independence in its internal and external activities, safeguard the purity of Marxism-Leninism against Right and "Left" opportunism, and abide by the principles contained in the Declaration and Statement of the meetings of representatives of the Communist and Workers parties of all countries. Our Party will endeavor to defend the unity of the socialist camp and solidarity of the international communist movement based on the principles of Marxism-Leninism and proletarian internationalism, oppose imperialism, and carry the revolution through to the end in close unity with the peoples of the whole world.

VIII.

CONSOLIDATION AND ADVANCE OF SOCIALISM

THE GREAT triumph of the Korean people in the struggle waged under the banner of the Republic over the past 20 years for the success and development of the country and the prosperity of the nation is due entirely to the fact that they have advanced vigorously along the socialist path, steadfastly relying on the indestructible vitality of socialism. Our triumph is striking proof of the superiority of the socialist system over the capitalist system.

The socialist system is a most advanced social system under which power is in the hands of the masses of the people, production is developed steadily in a planned way on a high scientific and technical foundation for the purpose of systematically enhancing the welfare of the people on the basis of the public ownership of the means of production, all kinds of exploitation and oppression have been abolished once and for all, and each works according to his ability and takes his share according to the quality and quantity of work done.

Unlike capitalist society where the people have neither political rights nor freedom, the socialist system substantially provides genuine democratic rights and freedom to the masses of the people in all spheres of politics, economy and culture. In our society, the entire people participate freely in the politics of the

From *The Democratic People's Republic of Korea is the Banner of Freedom and Independence for Our People and the Powerful Weapon For Building Socialism and Communism.* Report at the 20th Anniversary Celebration of the Founding of the DPRK, September 7, 1968.

country, exercise state power for their revolutionary cause, choose their occupations and professions according to their ability and aptitude, and work, study and live with full enjoyment. In capitalist society, where the means of production are private property and the aim of production is to squeeze out more profits for the capitalists and landed proprietors, the masses of the producers are obliged to work to keep body and soul together and have no interests in the development of production and technology. In socialist society, however, the means of production are public property and the working people work for the country and society and for themselves. This enables the masses of the people to give full play to their inexhaustible creative initiative and talents, to develop production steadily and swiftly. In socialist society all branches of the national economy and all enterprises are linked organically with each other on the basis of the community of aims and interests. So there is no anarchy of production and crises of overproduction as in capitalist society, the national economy develops according to plan and proportionately and all the manpower and material resources and the potentialities of production in the country can be tapped and turned to account most efficiently. Moreover, under the socialist system there exists neither exploiter nor exploited, the fruits of labor go entirely to the enhancement of the welfare of the working people, and the living standards of the people rise systematically with the rapid growth of production.

The capitalist path is the path of exploitation and oppression, slavery and ruin, while the socialist path is the path leading to the abolition of class exploitation and national oppression, to the freedom and happiness of the entire people, and to complete independence and prosperity of the country.

The two diametrically different realities in North and South Korea furnish a striking example. In the northern half of the Republic, the most progressive, socialist system has been established which is free from exploitation and oppression, the foundations of a powerful independent national economy have been laid, and the people enjoy genuine freedom and happiness, whereas South Korea has been turned into U.S. imperialism's colony and military base for aggression, its economy has been utterly dilapidated, and the people are groaning under terrorism and tyranny, deprived of all political freedom and even elementary democratic rights, and are suffering from hardships of life never known in thousands of years.

Historical experience shows that a people who have got rid of the colonial yoke of imperialism must take the socialist path. A people who have won independence should strive actively to crush the subversive maneuvers of foreign imperialism and domestic reactionary forces and tear down the colonial ruling machine of imperialism, demolish and wipe out the economic foothold of imperialism and domestic reaction, strengthen the revolutionary forces and establish a progressive social system, and build an independent national economy and national culture. This alone will enable them to advance dynamically along the shortcut to the freedom and happiness of the people and national independence and prosperity without repeating the bitter history of woe and distress which capitalism has inevitably inflicted.

Capitalism has already lived out its days and is rushing ever more precipitately along the road to its doom. Socialism and communism represent the bright future of mankind, and it is an inexorable law of historical development that all nations head for socialism and communism.

In future, too, we will continue to advance steadily along the socialist path without the slightest vacillation.

Our people are confronted today with the historic task of assuring the complete triumph of socialism by promoting more vigorously the revolution and socialist construction on the basis of the brilliant successes already achieved in the building of a new society.

We have built the firm basis of socialism in the northern half of the country. But we still have much more work to do to win complete victory for socialism. Even after building the basis of socialism the socialist state should continue to carry out the revolution thoroughly in all spheres of politics, economy and culture.

Even after the exploiting classes have been liquidated and the socialist reorganization of production relations completed, the class struggle continues over the whole period of transition from capitalism to socialism. It is true that when socialist reorganization is completed in town and country, the exploiting classes are liquidated completely as classes and their socio-economic foothold ceases to exist. But elements of those classes survive and endlessly perpetrate subversive activities without discarding the delusion of restoring their old positions. Even after the triumph of the socialist system, therefore, hostile elements remain for a long time in socialist society. Though insignificant in themselves, these hostile elements should never be ignored, for they are tools and agents of foreign imperialists. While resorting to direct armed intervention to oppose and invade the socialist countries, the imperialists maneuver to wreck the socialist countries from within by rallying and supporting the remnants of the overthrown exploiting classes and reactionaries in the socialist countries.

Especially in our country, U.S. imperialism, the chieftain of world reaction, is entrenched in South Korea, incessantly perpetrating activities of subversion, sabotage and ideological penetration, instigating the reactionary classes in the southern half and the remnant elements of the exploiting classes in the northern half to overthrow the socialist system in the North.

Even after the establishment of the socialist system, the residue of old thoughts left over from the ancient exploiter society survives for a long time in the minds of the working people. The triumph of the socialist system puts an end to the economic basis engendering outmoded thoughts and creates the social and material conditions for arming people with new ideas. But since the development of the ideological consciousness of people lags behind the change in the material conditions of society, the survivals of old ideas left over from the exploiter society persist long in the minds of the working people, even after the socialist system has triumphed. Also, the venom of bourgeois ideology infiltrates ceaselessly into socialist society from outside owing to ideological and cultural penetration by the imperialists.

At the same time, there remain distinctions between town and countryside and class distinctions between working class and peasantry for a long time after the undivided sway of socialist production relations has been established in the whole society. The lag of the countryside behind the towns is expressed above all in the fact that agriculture has a weaker material and technical foundation than industry, the cultural level of the rural population is lower than that of the urban dwellers, and the peasants fall behind the workers in ideological consciousness. This backwardness is a legacy of the old society. It is due to this backwardness that the cooperative economy remains the predominant form in agriculture, whereas public property rules supreme in industry and, accordingly, there remain the class distinctions between the working class and peasantry.

We have much to do in the way of developing the productive forces as well. By establishing the advanced, socialist system in the past years, we have paved a broad road for the development of the productive forces and the improvement of the people's living conditions. But we have merely laid the basis of industrialization and taken the first step in the technical revolution; we have yet a long way to go to attain a high level of productive forces commensurate with socialist and communist society. Also as concerns the people's livelihood we have eliminated the social sources of exploitation and poverty and developed production at a fast tempo, and thus solved the most essential problems in the material and cultural life of our people. But we have not yet been able to make their life very bountiful and cultured.

A society cannot yet be called a completely triumphant socialist society if the hostile classes persist in their insidious maneuvers, the corrosive action of old ideas continues, distinctions between town and countryside and class distinctions between working class and peasantry still remain, the industrialization of the country has not been realized fully and the material and technical basis of socialism has not been laid firmly.

In order to achieve the complete victory of socialism and accomplish the historical task of the working class, the socialist state must strengthen its role as a weapon of class struggle, a weapon for the building of socialism and communism. In other words, the socialist state should strengthen the dictatorship of the proletariat, carrying on the class struggle on the one hand and vigorously pushing ahead with the building of the socialist economy on the other.

Only when the socialist state acquits itself well both in exercising dictatorship against the hostile elements and in carrying out ideological revolution and economic work, can it occupy the two fortresses, ideological and material, which must be captured on the way to socialism and communism, to guarantee complete triumph for socialism. If either of these tasks is neglected or overlooked, it will cause great difficulties and irretrievably grave losses along the whole course of socialist construction.

If the socialist state neglects the dictatorship of the proletariat and ideological revolution to the slightest degree and slackens the class struggle, it will become impossible to consolidate and develop the triumphant socialist system or defend it against the encroachment of internal and external enemies. The intrinsic superiority of socialism and its great vitality lie above all in the fact that the working people freed from exploitation and oppression unite firmly and cooperate closely with each other as comrades and display creative initiative and voluntary zeal in their work for the common goal and interests. Experience shows that without stimulating the class awakening and raising the level of ideological consciousness of the working people by intensifying the class struggle, the superiority of socialism cannot emerge and the working people fall victim to indolence and slackness, thereby making it impossible to carry out the tasks of economic construction and technical revolution successfully.

On the other hand, it is also wrong to stress only the class struggle and ideological revolution and slight the building of socialist economy. Though the ideological revolution is an important revolutionary task which the socialist state must carry out without fail, it is not an end in itself. The ideological revolution aims to root out the old thoughts remaining in the minds of the working people and to call forth their voluntary zeal and creative initiative so as to build socialism and communism successfully. Communists not only fight for the freedom and liberation of the people but also strive to assure them a happy life. An important task which confronts the Communists after they have overthrown the old system and liberated the people from exploitation and oppression, is to build the socialist economy well. Concern for improving the welfare of the people is the supreme principle governing the activities of the Party and state of the working class. Our struggle for the building of socialism and communism is aimed, in the final analysis, at satisfying fully the material and cultural requirements of all the people and ensuring them a bountiful and cultured life. Only when economic construction is done well, can the high level of development of the productive forces be attained which corresponds to socialist and communist society, the country be made rich and strong, and the livelihood of the people be raised decisively. And only when the material and technical basis of socialism is well laid by vigorously promoting economic construction, can the political independence and sovereignty of the country be secured firmly and its defense potentials also strengthened.

If stress is put only on the idsological revolution and the technical revolution is neglected, the revolutionary task of relieving the working people from arduous labor cannot be accomplished, nor can the ideological revolution itself be carried out successfully. The ideological consciousness of people is determined by the material conditions of social life; so in socialist society, too, it is transformed as technology develops and the people's living standards rise.

Guarding against all kinds of Right and "Left" deviations which might arise here, we should strengthen continuously the dictatorship of the proletariat and the class struggle and also carry on economic construction efficiently, and should give definite precedence to the ideological revolution while at the same time pushing ahead energetically with the technical revolution. Only by so doing is it possible to remold the ideology of people, and build the solid material and technical foundations of socialism and thus achieve the complete victory of socialism.

First of all, we should strengthen the dictatorship over the class enemy, and carry out thoroughly the ideological revolution to revolutionize and "working-classize"* the whole of society.

The historical mission of the dictatorship of the proletariat lies in educating and remolding all working people, to revolutionize and "working-classize" them, in gradually eliminating all class distinctions, and in building communism while liquidating the exploiting classes and putting down their resistance. We should properly combine the Party's class line and mass line to isolate and suppress a handful of hostile elements and, at the same time, educate and remold the broad masses to rally them closer around the Party.

As you all know, the dictatorship of the proletariat means on the one hand suppression of the few hostile elements and on the other democracy for the absolute majority of the population—the working class, peasantry and other sections of the working people. To link correctly these two aspects of the proletarian dictatorship means properly to combine the work of uniting, through education and remolding, the absolute majority of the masses of the people around the class struggle against the intrigues and maneuvers of the very few hostile elements. A "Leftist" error will be committed if only the class struggle is emphasized and exaggerated, forgetting that the unity and co-operation of the working class, peasantry and working intelligentsia constitute the basis of social relations in socialist society. In that case, one may tend to distrust people, treat innocent people as hostile elements, divorce the Party from the masses and cause unrest in society.

In contrast, a grave Rightist error will be committed if so-called "democracy" is exercised for all people and "freedom" is granted to them in disregard of the fact that in socialist society, too, there exist hostile elements, survivals of old ideology remain

---

*The term "working-classize" has been adopted by the editors of works published in English in Korea and has also been retained in Western editions of these works. It is used here in quotation marks to indicate the term has been coined to convey the particular meaning it has come to have in the ideological revolution as defined by Kim Il Sung.

and class struggle continues. Democracy as a political concept intrinsically assumes class character. The dictatorship of all exploiters is a dictatorship over the exploited laboring masses and their democracy is a democracy solely for the few exploiters. On the other hand, the dictatorship of the proletariat is a dictatorship over the exploiting classes and a democracy for the broad masses of the people. As there has been no state detached from classes in the history of mankind, so there is and can be no democracy which does not bear a class character. In any state, democracy is a democracy for the class that has seized power, and is combined with the dictatorship over the hostile classes. Under conditions in which remnant elements of the overthrown exploiting classes maneuver insidiously and class struggle continues, there can be no "pure democracy" or "complete freedom" for all. Bourgeois democracy provides the billionaires with the freedom of exploiting and plundering the working people for profit and of oppressing them at will, but it allows only the freedom of wearing rags and starving to death to the toiling masses. If the class character of democracy is denied in socialist society and so-called "pure democracy" and "complete freedom" for all under the dictatorship of the proletariat are advocated, it is, in fact, tantamount to forcing bourgeois democracy and slavish freedom upon the people. We are against an abstract and supra-class comprehension of democracy.

Now the Western imperialists and the renegades of revolution are cheering so-called "democratic development" and "liberalization" in some socialist countries, describing them as a "lawful process" of the development of socialist society, a "new wind in Eastern Europe that brings hope to the Western world," a "deep-going process of transformation for further democracy," and so on. This is, after all, a foolish maneuver of the imperialists and the renegades of revolution to encroach upon socialist gains and open the way to the restoration of capitalism in the socialist countries. We should heighten vigilance against the intrigues and maneuvers of the imperialists to subvert the socialist countries from within.

If the peoples of the socialist countries are to enjoy genuine freedom and democracy, the dictatorship of the proletariat should be strengthened. The content of proletarian democracy is to liquidate the exploiting classes forever, assure not only true political freedom and rights in full but also a happy material and cultural life to the working class and other sections of the working people, and to strengthen comradely cooperation and assistance among them in every way. There can be no better democracy than proletarian democracy. Should there be any higher form of democracy than proletarian democracy, it is no longer a democracy. It is wrong to think that the dictatorship of the proletariat has become unnecessary even before class distinctions between the working class and peasantry are obliterated, before ideological survivals of the old society are eradicated, and particularly at a time when enemies at home and abroad continue to intensify their aggressive and subversive activities against socialism. Should we shirk a principled class struggle, obscuring the class line between bourgeois democracy and proletarian democracy and negating the class character of democracy, vigilance against hostile elements may grow dull, the leading role of the Party and the working class be paralyzed, and the corrosive action of the bourgeoisie intensified in social life.

In fine, both the Right and "Left" deviations make it impossible to distinguish clearly friend from foe, and cause great losses to the construction of socialism and communism. It is a consistent line of our Party properly to combine the dictatorship with democracy, and class struggle with the work of strengthening the unity and cohesion of the masses of the people, while opposing all Right and "Left" deviations in state activities.

We should in the future also continue to heighten the functions of proletarian dictatorship, thereby successfully frustrating all kinds of intrigues and maneuvers of the enemies within and without against our socialist system. We should apply strict sanctions against the remnants of the overthrown classes of landlords and capitalists who still do not give up the dream of restoring their old positions, and we should make a resolute counter-attack and smash to bits in good time the counter-revolutionary attempts of the imperialists to attack our social system in collusion with the hostile elements within. We should thus defend the gains of our revolution firmly and guarantee reliably the complete victory of socialism in our country.

While suppressing the hostile elements, we should intensify the leading role of the working class over all social strata and carry out the ideological revolution thoroughly, thus revolutionizing and "working-classizing" all members of society.

True, suppression of the hostile elements is the basic function of the state of the proletarian dictatorship and a form of class struggle which the socialist state should carry out to the end, but that does not comprise all functions of proletarian dictatorship nor all forms of class struggle. Besides the class struggle to suppress hostile elements, there is the basic form of class struggle in socialist society whose major content is the ideological revolution to root out the obsolete ideas in the minds of the working people and arm them with communist ideas. Even after the triumph of the socialist system the class struggle continues, but it should be somewhat different in content and form.

Indeed, the struggle against the survivals of old ideas in the minds of the working people in socialist society is a class struggle in that it is a struggle between working-class ideology and bourgeois ideology, but it is entirely different from the previous class struggle. The class struggle during the socialist revolution was primarily a struggle for complete liquidation of the exploiters as a class, whereas the class struggle after the establishment of the socialist system is not designed to liquidate people but is primarily an ideological struggle to remold their thoughts. The ideological revolution in socialist society is an internal affair of the working people who advance hand in hand to attain the common ideal, and is aimed at educating and remolding all working people into Communists. The ideological revolution should be carried out not by force as in the struggle against hostile elements, but always by means of persuasion and education and it should be linked with the work of cementing the unity and cohesion of the working people.

In socialist society the main objects of the ideological revolution are the remnants of old feudal, bourgeois and petty-bourgeois ideas in the minds of the working people and the virus of reactionary capitalist ideology infiltrating from outside. The socialist state should unfold vigorously the ideological revolution to root out all survivals of old ideas and thoroughly prevent the penetration of the poison of bourgeois ideology from outside. Especially in our situation, where the country remains divided and we are confronted directly with U.S. imperialism, the chieftain of world reaction, the struggle against subversion, sabotage and ideological infiltration acquires a greater importance, to which we should always pay serious attention. While steadily enhancing the leading role of the working class, we should conduct persistent education in the Party's policies and revolutionary traditions, communist education with class education as its basic content, and education in socialist patriotism, thereby revolutionizing and "working-classizing" all the working people.

To solve the rural question and raise cooperative property to the level of public property is one of the most important tasks confronting the state of the proletarian dictatorship after the triumph of the socialist system and one of the basic conditions for the complete victory of socialism. Only when the rural question is solved completely and the backwardness of the countryside is eliminated, can the socialist state make a clean sweep of the soil in which the reactionary bourgeois virus coming from outside and the remnants of the overthrown exploiting classes may take root. And only when cooperative property is raised to the level of public property, can the agricultural productive forces be developed to a high degree, the elements of selfish ideology remaining in the minds of the peasants be rooted out, and all working people be led without deviating along the path of collectivism to work for the whole of society and the entire people with a high degree of conscious zeal.

Our Party, generalizing the achievements and experience gained in rural work, has already set forth the basic principle and concrete way to solve the rural question in socialist society. In accordance with the clear-cut line set by the Party, we should step up energetically the technical, cultural and ideological revolutions in the countryside to put an end to the technical lag of argriculture behind modern industry, the cultural backwardness of the countryside in comparison with the advanced towns, and the ideological lag of the peasantry behind the working class, the most revolutionary class. We should continue to strengthen leadership and assistance to the rural areas by the Party and state of the working class, and develop public property and cooperative property in organic combination, while steadily bringing the latter closer to the former.

To win complete victory for socialism, economic construction should be promoted vigorously, while every class distinction is eliminated and cooperative property is elevated to the level of public property. Our task in the domain of socialist economic construction is to carry through the industrialization of the country and the technical and cultural revolutions so that the material and technical foundations of socialism may be laid solidly and all the working people may master the know-how and skills to handle up-to-date machines efficiently.

We should develop industry continuously at a fast rate and equip all branches of the national economy, including agriculture, with modern techniques, thus building a modern industry and a developed agriculture in our country. We should develop all people into all-around, competent builders of communism. In this way we should relieve our people, who have rid themselves of exploitation, from arduous labor and gradually obliterate the distinctions between industrial and agricultural labor, heavy and light labor, physical and mental labor, so that they may produce more material wealth with less expenditure of labor. On the basis of speedily developing industrial and agricultural production we should raise the material and cultural standards of all working people at least to the living standard of the middle classes in the past, and above that. Thus, it must be assured that all people feel the real superiority of the socialist system more keenly in their actual life, fighting with devotion for the consolidation and development of the socialist system, firmly confident of the complete victory of socialism. Only when this is realized can we say the triumph of socialism is complete.

IX.

ON SOME THEORETICAL PROBLEMS OF THE SOCIALIST ECONOMY

IN APRIL 1968 I received questions from scholars, through the Science and Education Department of the Party Central Committee, concerning some problems of socialist economic theory. But, as the situation in the country was tense and we had the celebrations of the 20th anniversary of the foundation of the Republic last year, I had little time to spare for a prompt answer to the questions. I was told that even until now some leading economic functionaries and scholars have no clear idea of these problems and are arguing about them. Therefore, I am now going to give my opinion about them.

1. PROBLEM OF THE CORRELATION BETWEEN THE SCALE OF THE ECONOMY AND THE RATE OF DEVELOPMENT OF PRODUCTION

Of late a theory is in vogue among certain economists that though the economy grows without interruption in socialist society, its rate of growth cannot exceed 4-5 or 6-7 per cent a year when the economy reaches a certain stage of development. I was told there are also people among the leading workers of our state economic bodies who argue that should our industrial output increase even only by 6-7 per cent a year, it would be high enough, inasmuch as in capitalist countries production rises barely by 2-3 per cent a year.

Answers to the questions raised by scientific and educational workers. March 1, 1969 (in full).

They base such an argument on the assumption that the reserves for production growth diminish in the period of reconstruction as compared with the period of rehabilitation and that, accordingly, the more the economy develops and its scale grows, the less becomes the possibility of increasing production. In other words, they contend that the further industry advances, the more the reserves are reduced and the slower becomes the rate of production growth. In our country, too, they say, there were plenty of reserves in the postwar rehabilitation period, but today when the basis of socialist industrialization has been laid and we are in the period of an all-out technical reconstruction of the national economy, production cannot be multiplied at an ever higher rate, for there exist no such reserves.

People who think this way either are not aware of the true advantages of the socialist economic system or are unwilling to see them.

Socialist society has unlimited potentialities to develop the economy incessantly at such a high rate as is inconceivable in capitalist society, and the further socialist construction advances and the stronger the economic base grows the greater become these potentials.

In capitalist society production cannot grow steadily, the process of reproduction being periodically interrupted and much social labor wasted owing to crises of overproduction. In socialist society, however, all the labor resources and natural wealth of the country can be utilized most reasonably and production can be raised constantly according to plan. This possibility of production growth will always increase providing equilibrium among branches of the national economy is rationally preserved and the country's economy is kept in ever better shape with the strengthening of the economy-organizing functions of the state of the proletarian dictatorship and the rise in the level of economic management of the functionaries. Since the socialist state controls by coordination, and realizes production and distribution, accumulation and consumption according to plan, it can allocate a large amount of funds to accumulation and carry on socialist extended reproduction steadily on a big scale by using the funds most reasonably.

And the production relations of socialism open a wide scope for an unrestricted development of the productive forces; the socialist state, by making use of this possibility, can rapidly develop technology according to plan. It is a law-governed process of building socialism and communism that outmoded technique be replaced by new technique and the new by a yet newer one, that manual labor be mechanized, mechanization develop to semi-automation, and semi-automation to automation. It is a palpable truth that in socialist society, with the rapid development of technology, labor productivity increases constantly and production develops at a high rate.

In socialist society, the people's high revolutionary zeal is the decisive factor which causes the productive forces to multiply. The essential excellence of the socialist system lies in the fact that the working people, freed from exploitation and oppression, work with conscious enthusiasm and creative initiative for the country and the people, for society and the collective, as well as their own welfare. In capitalist society the working people are not at all interested in the development of production and technology, for they work of necessity under the menace of unemployment and hunger. But in socialist society the working people work zealously for the development of production, because they are deeply aware that the fruits of their labor belong to themselves, to their people and their country. The more the Party and state of the proletariat, in conformity with their proper functions, strengthen the ideological revolution among the working people and gradually eliminate the survivals of old ideologies from their minds, the more the working people will devote their talents and energy to the development of socialist production. In this way, continuous improvement and innovation will be brought about in all fields of economic management, organization of production and labor, and development of technology.

All this testifies to the utter fallacy of the theory that in socialist society the reserves for increased production diminish gradually and production cannot be kept rising at a high rate as the economy develops and its scale expands.

Practical experiences in building socialism in our country also irrefutably prove that such a theory is wrong.

To begin with, let me tell you what happened when we were tackling the Five-Year Plan. The economic life of our country at that time was very hard in general, although our Party members and working people in the main had rehabilitated the ravaged economy and made the living of the people stable by carrying out successfully the Three-Year National Economic Plan. Moreover, enemies at home and abroad were running amuck to encroach upon the gains of our revolution and ruin the constructive work of our people. Under such circumstances we were confronted with the urgent task of quickly laying the foundation of industrialization to advance the economy of the country and improve the people's livelihood. This required large quantities of rolled steel.

But at that time our country had only one blooming mill and its rated capacity was no more than 60,000 tons. Sixty thousand tons of rolled steel were, however, far from enough, for we had to build town and country, erect factories, and turn out more machines.

In all previous arduous, revolutionary struggles our Party had trusted the working class and, leaning upon their strength, broke through bottlenecks and difficulties. And this time, too, our Party decided to go to the working class, consult them and overcome existing difficulties.

Entrusted by the GPolitical Committee of the Party Central Committee, we went to the Kangson Steel Works. When we asked the leading personnel of that plant if they could not increase the output of rolled steel to 90,000 tons, some of them, shaking their heads, said that it would be difficult. So we called the workers together and told them: We have barely managed to rehabilitate the ravaged economy, and now the factionalists have reared their heads against the Party and the great-power chauvinists put pressure on us, and the U.S. imperialists and the Syngman Rhee puppet clique are getting frantic with "march north" clamors. But can all that be any excuse for us to get disheartened and yield to the grave difficulties lying in the way of the cause of revolution and construction? No, that won't do. We only trust you, the working class, the main force of our revolution, and we have no one but you to rely on. Then, to tide over these grave difficulties facing our Party, you must be in high spirits and work hard to produce plenty and construct well, and thus drive economic construction more vigorously, isn't that so?

We conducted our political work in this way, and the workers of Kangson came out with a resolution to produce 90,000 tons of rolled steel. Roused to activity, they strove hard, improving existing machines and equipment and undoing knots, with the result that 120,000 tons of rolled steel was turned out instead of 90,000 that year. This steel works could raise the capacity of the bloomery to the present level of 450,000 tons, that is, nearly eight times the rated capacity.

Not only in the Kangson Steel Works but in all fields of the national economy and all factories and enterprises, the old rated capacities were scrapped and great innovations were made, miracles wrought day after day to startle the world, and the economy of our country developed at a very high rate. Thus, the Five-Year Plan envisaging a 2.6-fold increase in total industrial output value was carried out in two years and a half, and the production plan for major manufactured goods was also fulfilled or overfulfilled in all indices of products in four years.

During the last seven or eight years since the fulfilment of the Five-Year Plan, the tasks of the overall technical revolution have been carried forward vigorously in our country with the result that a number of new fields of industry have been opened, the technical equipment of industry has been improved radically, and the scale of production expanded many times. If the "theory" of some people were right, that with the expansion of the scale of production the rate of its growth decreases, it would have been impossible for our country to keep up the high tempo of production growth in the period that followed the fulfilment of the Five-Year Plan. But in the Seven-Year Plan period, too, the economy has developed constantly at a high speed, though our country appropriated a large part of accumulation additionally for the defense buildup in view of the more pronounced aggressive maneuvers of the U.S. imperialists.

Thus the National Economic Plan for 1967, the first year for implementing the decision of the Party Conference on building the economy and defense at the same time, was a tight plan, envisaging an increase of 12.8 per cent in the value of total industrial output over the previous year. But in 1967 we actually overfulfilled the plan by far and raised industrial output as much as 17 per cent in a year. Had it not been for the rare flood damage that year, industrial output would have risen more than 20 per cent. This is to be ascribed to the fact that our Party intensified the ideological revolution among the working people, thereby arousing their enthusiasm, and waged a resolute struggle against passivism, conservatism and all kinds of antiquated ideas that hampered our forward movement.

Take the Songhung Mine for example.

In 1967 when the managing personnel of the Songhung Mine came up with a plan setting a very low target, the Cabinet persuaded them to raise it a little higher. Yet, even this was too low to meet the demand of the Party. So the Party Central Committee, with a view to conducting political work among the workers of the Songhung Mine, summoned the cadres of the mine, platoon leaders and others to a meeting. There, we told them: To carry out successfully the line of building the economy and defense in parallel as set forth by the Party Conference, the Songhung Mine will have to extract more nonferrous metal. Thereupon, they pledged themselves to exceed the target set by the Cabinet. In the end, they produced nearly twice as much as they had promised at first.

Let us take another example. Functionaries in the engineering industry said they had no reserve, so we went to the Ryongsong Machine Plant in 1967 and kindled the drive for innovation. The workers there responded and fulfilled the keyed-up plan for the year, including the plan for extra production, by October 10, two months and 20 days ahead of schedule.

Great reserves were also found in the course of the struggle to carry out last year's national economic plan.

In view of the frantic war cries by the U.S. imperialists following the *Pueblo** incident, the Party Central Committee addressed an appeal last year to factories and enterprises in all fields of the national economy to fulfil ahead of schedule all assignments of production and construction and produce more with the additional labor power, materials and equipment at their disposal.

This revolutionary call of the Party found a response in all factories and enterprises, and many of them, out of a burning desire to drive the U.S. imperialists from our soil and unify the country at the earliest possible date, asked for more assignments and carried out their resolve very well.

All this shows that we can develop the economy as fast as we want, no matter how big its scale, if by conducting political work well in accordance with the line set forth by our Party, we enhance the political consciousness of the masses, arouse their revolutionary zeal and constantly improve techniques.

The "theory" that once industry reaches a certain stage of development the reserves diminish and a high rate of growth can not be assured in industrial production, has nothing to do with Marxist-Leninist economic theory. The "theory" that large-scale economy can not develop rapidly is but a sophistry brought forward by some people to justify the fact that their technical progress is slow and their economy stagnant because they, talking about "liberalization" and "democratic development," did not educate their working people and, as a result, the latter are ideologically so soft as to fiddle about and loaf on the job.

Referring to the immediate tasks of Soviet power after the victory of the October Socialist Revolution, Lenin put forward the famous proposition: Communism is Soviet power plus the electrification of the whole country. This proposition of Lenin's, though simple, has a profound meaning. I think it is of great importance for building socialism and communism that we have a correct understanding of this proposition and translate it into practice. What is meant by the Soviet power mentioned by

*In January 1968, the *Pueblo*, a U.S. spy ship which had intruded into North Korean waters, was captured with its crew by the armed forces of the DPRK.

Lenin? It means no less than the dictatorship of the proletariat. It, therefore, means that the state of the working class should continue the class struggle and carry out the ideological and cultural revolutions to remold the consciousness of the people, raise their technical and cultural level, and accomplish the task of "working-classizing" and revolutionizing the whole of society. By electrification is meant that technology should be developed to such a high level as to make possible the automation of all production processes, greatly consolidating the material production basis of society. To sum up, this proposition of Lenin's teaches that communism will be realized only when the dictatorship of the proletariat is strengthened to accomplish the ideological and cultural revolutions and to revolutionize and "working-classize" the whole of society; and, at the same time, as the technical revolution is accomplished, to lay a solid material and technical basis for a very high level of productive forces.

If we neglect one or the other—the dictatorship of the proletariat or the technical revolution alluded to by Lenin—we can neither develop steadily the socialist economy at a high tempo nor build a communist society. We should therefore strengthen the dictatorship of the proletariat and pursue the technical revolution dynamically to build a communist society. As Lenin passed away before he himself could build communism, we must give a correct interpretation to his proposition and carry it into effect. Some people, however, refuse correctly to understand and put into effect this proposition of Lenin's. We must oppose categorically Right opportunism in the field of economic theory in order to accelerate socialist construction at a higher rate. If we do not take issue with the Right deviation in the economic field, if we weaken the proletarian dictatorship, fail to conduct political work and foster individual selfishness among the people, trying to make the people move merely with a money incentive, we cannot call forth their collective heroism and inventive initiative; accordingly, we cannot carry out successfully the tasks either of technical revolution or of economic construction. If we tail after the Right opportunist theory and fail to develop the economy rapidly, we may find it difficult even to provide everybody with a job and feed him. Then, how can we who have taken over very backward productive forces from the old society, catch up with the advanced countries and build a communist society where each works according to his ability and each receives according to his needs? We must reject the Right opportunist theory, definitely defend and carry through to the end the revolutionary ideas of our Party, the theory of economic construction of our Party, and thus keep on the grand march of Chollima in building socialism.

2. PROBLEMS OF MEANS OF PRODUCTION AS A COMMODITY AND THE USE OF THE LAW OF VALUE

I have heard that some economists are arguing about the questions of whether or not the means of production is a commodity in socialist society and whether or not the law of value operates in the domain of its production and circulation.

I think these questions should not be handled in the same breath. In socialist society the means of production can sometimes be a commodity and sometimes not, as the case may be. So, the law of value will operate when it is a commodity, and will not when it is not, because the law of value is a law of commodity production.

When is the means of production a commodity and when is it not? To find the right solution to this question I deem it necessary, first of all, to have a clear idea of the properties of a commodity and the origin of commodity production.

A commodity is a thing produced not for one's own consumption but for sale. In other words, not all products are commodities, but things produced for the purpose of exchange are commodities. Thus for a product to be a commodity, there must be: (1) the social division of labor through which different kinds of goods are produced; (2) the seller and the buyer—the one who gives up the right to possess a thing by selling it and the other who buys and acquires the right to possess it. That is to say, commodity production presupposes the social division of labor and the differentiation of ownership of the product. Therefore, where there is no social division of labor and ownership is not differentiated but remains in a single form, there can be no commodity production.

The reason why commodity-money relations exist in socialist society can also be explained by the fact that there exist the social division of labor and different forms of ownership of the product. As everybody knows, in socialist society the division of labor not only exists but develops every day. As for ownership, there exist state and cooperative ownership of the means of production and the private ownership of consumer goods as well, though in the course of the socialist revolution private ownership is abolished and different forms of economy that existed in the early part of the transition period are gradually fused into a single, socialist form of economy. Besides, socialist states must carry on foreign trade under the circumstances that communism has not yet triumphed on a worldwide scale and frontiers exist.

All these factors give rise to commodity production in socialist society. It goes without saying that in socialist society commodity production is a production of goods without the capitalist and, therefore, the law of value operates not blindly as in capitalist society but within a limited scope, and the state uses it in a planned way as an economic lever for effective management of the economy. Later, when the transition period is over and cooperative property is turned into property of the entire people so that a unitary form of ownership is established, the produce of society, if foreign trade is not taken into consideration, will be called not by the name of commodity but simply means of production and consumer goods or by some other names. Then, the law of value will also cease to operate. Needless to say, even then the social division of labor will continue to develop, but commodity production will no longer exist.

Scholars, leading economic functionaries and many other people now commit Right or "Left" errors in both the theoretical domain and in economic management because they have not fully understood whether the means of production is a commodity or not in socialist society. As a result, some fall into the Right tendency to manage the economy in a capitalist way, overrating the importance of commodity production and the law of value in the wake of revisionist theory. Others commit the "ultra-Left" error of failing to streamline management of enterprise, and causing a large waste of means of production and labor power by totally ignoring commodity production and the role of the law of value in disregard of the transitional character of our society. A correct understanding of this question and of how to deal with it is of weighty importance in socialist economic construction. After all, the question of utilizing commodity-money relations is an important one which the state of the working class must properly settle in the period of transition from capitalism to socialism. Right or "Left" error on this question can cause serious harm.

The distinction between the means of production as a commodity and as a non-commodity in socialist society is to be found in the differentiation of ownership. In socialist society the means of production, even when shifted from one place to another, is not a commodity as long as it does not change hands, and it is a commodity when it changes hands. Obvious conclusions are to be derived from this, as follows:

(1) When a means of production turned out in the state sector of ownership is transferred to cooperative ownership or vice versa, it is a commodity in either case and, therefore, the law of value operates here. (2) A means of production which is exchanged within the bounds of cooperative ownership—between cooperative farms, between producers' cooperatives or between the former and the latter—is equally a commodity and here, too, the law of value operates. (3) In the case of export the means of production is a commodity and it is exchanged at the world market price or at the socialist market price. For instance, when countries like Indonesia and Cambodia ask our country for machine tools, the machine tools sold to these countries are commodities for which we should receive due prices. And when a confederation of the North and the South, though not yet realized at the moment, is established in our country in accordance with our Party's proposal for national unification, and businessmen in South Korea ask us for machines and equipment, the machines

and equipment we shall sell them will be commodities, and here the law of value will necessarily come into consideration.

What, then, are the equipment, raw and other materials that are transferred from one state enterprise to another? They are not commodities. Because means of production such as these are turned out on the basis of socialist cooperation in production, and even when they are transferred from one enterprise to another, they remain under the ownership of the socialist state, and such means of production are supplied not through free trade but in a planned way by the state according to the plan of equipment and material supply. When the state finds it necessary, it provides the enterprises with the means of production, even if the enterprises do not ask for them, just as it provides the army with weapons. The machines, equipment, raw and other materials transferred from one state enterprise to another, therefore, cannot be called commodities, realized through the operation of the law of value.

Then, what shall we call these means of production turned over from one state enterprise to another, if not commodities, and what shall we say is being made use of, if not the operation of the law of value, in assessing the prices of the means of production when they are transferred, or in accounting their costs when produced? It would be right to say that the means of production which are transferred between the state enterprises according to the plans of equipment and material supply and of cooperative production are not commodities, but assume the form of commodity, and, accordingly, that in this case the law of value does not operate in substance as in the case of commodity production, but in form.

In other words, such means of production are not commodities in the proper sense of the word, but merely assume the form of commodity, and accordingly, what is made use of here is not the operation of the law of value in the proper sense of the word, but the law of value in form; and in the case of the production and exchange of the means of production, the form of value is made use of simply as an instrument of economic accounting, and does not represent the value itself.

Then, how are we going to explain that such means of production are not commodities but merely assume the form of commodity? It is so because state enterprises are relatively independent in using and managing the means of production and in running the economy, as if they were under different ownership, though they are all under one and the same ownership of the state. Though all the business-accounting enterprises in the state sector are owned by the state, they separately use the means of production received from other enterprises according to the unitary plan of the state, and must net a certain profit for the state after they recover the costs spent on their products.

Although such business-accounting state enterprises are under the same ownership, independence in management of each of them gives the impression that the means of production exchanged between them are commodities like those handed over to different ownership. Thus, when an enterprise delivers means of production to another, it does not give them free or dirt-cheap at random, but hands them over at prices fixed by the state uniformly according to the expenditure of socially necessary labor on the principle of equivalent compensation, though they are business-accounting enterprises in the state sector. Though equally state-owned, the enterprises have to be particular about things of their own and of others, and transactions in the means of production have to be conducted on a strict accounting basis.

Why, then, should enterprises within the state sector be granted independence in management, and why should a means of production be delivered and received by them with strict accounting on the principle of equivalence, when it is no commodity? That has something to do with the specific feature of socialist society which is a transitional one. In socialist society the productive forces have not yet developed to such an extent as to make it possible for each to work according to his ability and to receive according to his needs. And not all people possess so high a degree of collectivist spirit as to hold dear and take responsible care of state properties as if they were their own. In not a few cases, even those who are educated enough do not care as much about the business of other state bodies or enterprises as about their own, nor do they devote themselves to it, to say nothing of those who still harbor such ideological debris as wanting to impinge upon the interests of the state or other organs and enterprises, placing the narrow interests of their own organs and localities before everything, being stodgily departmentalized and parochialized. Further, under socialism labor has become, of course, honorable and worthwhile, but not yet life's prime requirement as in communist society. Thus, all these things require that under socialism equivalent values be strictly accounted in transactions between the enterprises, though they are all state-owned. If our society had a great affluence of goods and if the managing staffs and working people of all enterprises were free from selfishness, were as concerned about all state properties as about their own, and conducted all state affairs as devotedly as their own, then there would be no need of arranging accounts on an equivalent basis.

A proper use of the commodity form and the commercial form in the production and circulation of the means of production is of definite significance in methodically increasing the profits of enterprises and the accumulations of the state by eliminating the waste of social labor and strengthening the save-and-spare system. It is therefore necessary to make a proper use of them in all branches of the national economy and at all enterprises.

Above all, efforts should be made to use properly the form of value in the manufacture of the means of production to strengthen the strict accounting system and the control by *won* over the use of raw and other materials as well as labor power, systematically lowering the standard of material consumption per unit.

In the domain of circulation, too, the commercial form should be utilized fully, while good plans of equipment and material supply are mapped out, so as to do away with the waste of machines, equipment, and materials and use them in a rational way. When we set up the material supply agencies and saw to it that raw and other materials were bought and sold through the medium of the agencies, we aimed at assuring their smooth supply.

Our economic functionaries, however, fail to do this properly. The textbook of political economy, too, simply says that the means of production is excluded from the sphere of commodity circulation and is supplied to enterprises according to plan, but it makes no mention whatever of how and in what form its supply is realized. The question of supply of means of production is all but left out from the textbook of political economy; particularly, the question of purchase and sale of raw and other materials among state enterprises is not even touched upon.

Such being the case, many shortcomings have appeared in the supply of materials. When securing raw and other materials, the enterprises take them without caring much about their prices, high or low. Moreover, it is not infrequent that valuable materials lie idle in heaps at some enterprises, while at others production is interrupted for want of the same materials.

True, this is owing partly to defective plans of material supply mapped out by the State Planning Commission, but the issue lies rather in the ignorance of the fact that the supply of raw and other materials is also realized in the form of trade. That is to say, the supply of materials is realized in the form of commodity circulation, inasmuch as the form of selling and buying is adopted between state enterprises, too. But this has been ignored. As a result, should the planning organs map out erroneous plans for the supply of materials, nobody is to answer for the materials being kept idle or wasted, and the defect is detected nowhere.

To straighten out this question it is necessary, first of all, to enhance the role of the material supply agencies. When these agencies do their work well, they will not be besieged by crowds of people coming to procure materials and will be able properly to supply enterprises in need of them for effective use; the enterprises, on their part, will stop receiving materials at random with no consideration whatever of whether they are necessary or not, only to keep them idle or waste them.

We must know that when means of production such as machines, equipment and materials—while remaining under state ownership—are exchanged among enterprises, this is in the form of commodity circulation. Then, their prices will become an issue and so, if there sometimes happen to be defects in the plans, it will be possible to straighten them out in the course of actual supply.

Of course, in our society everything is produced, supplied, and consumed according to plan. Moreover, under the ownership of the entire people production, supply and consumption are completely planned. It is by no means easy, however, to have everything correctly planned. We have been carrying on a planned economy for over 20 years and we have kept on emphasizing that the plans must be objective. But planning is still not quite in order.

The same is true of the plan for supply of raw and other materials. Some kinds of materials are left out and some unnecessary things are included in the plan for supply. Where, then should the defects be detected? They should be detected at the supply agencies. That is, the plan must be complemented and corrected in the course of selling and buying raw and other materials through the agencies.

Besides, even if a material supply plan has been correctly drawn up, it cannot be executed when the supply work is not actually carried on properly. If the form of trade, that is, the form of selling and buying, is ignored in the supply of materials and if they are supplied simply according to plan, materials may be used at random and squandered at the enterprises. Such practices can take place quite often so long as our functionaries and working people are not all communist.

It is therefore necessary to raise the role of the supply agencies and make the most of the form of commodity circulation in the supply of raw and other materials. Thus, things must be so arranged that if an enterprise should over-purchase some kinds of materials it would not be able to buy other kinds, and if materials should be wasted, the business activities of the enterprise would be greatly affected. Only when such conditions are arranged in the supply of materials, will the functionaries of the enterprises come to check up closely the prices of materials and transport costs, value and take better care of materials, and make efforts to lower the standard of consumption per unit in the use of materials.

Now I should like to present my views on the question of making proper use of the law of value in the production and circulation of commodities.

Most important in the use of the law of value is to fix the prices of commodities properly. Prices should be assessed on the basis of correctly reckoning with the requirements of the basic economic law of socialism and the law of value.

First of all, the assessment of prices should be based correctly on the socially necessary labor contained in goods. If the fixing of prices is not based on the outlays of socially necessary labor, equilibrium of prices cannot be maintained, nor can socialist distribution take place properly, and the development of social production can be affected unfavorably.

Let us take an example. Once I walked into a shop in Changsong county of North Pyongan province, and I found there a meter of twisted-yarn fabric woven with 200 grams of yarn priced three *won* and a ball of thread weighing 50 grams at 5.4 *won*. It meant that a ball of thread was priced twice as high as a piece of cloth made of twisted yarn equivalent to four balls of thread, which was woven into fabric and dyed. Indeed, it seems to me that much labor and fairly large production costs were needed to reel thread at a local industry factory, because it was poorly mechanized. But since thread is not reeled by the hand-spinning-wheel, its cost cannot be greater than the cost of fabrics. And even if production costs were so high, the price cannot be fixed without taking into account the expenditure of socially necessary labor, and it goes against reason to fix the price so preposterously.

Further, low prices should be assigned to mass consumption goods when the prices are fixed. It is a matter of course, as I have mentioned above, that the values of commodities should be taken into account in assessing their prices. But this by no means signifies that the price of a commodity cannot be deviated from its value. The Party and the state of the working class should assign low prices to mass consumption goods by purposely deviating the prices of commodities from their values. That is to say, rice, cloth, footwear, mosquito nets, thread, matches, school things and other goods indispensable for the people's material and cultural life should be cheap. This means precisely a proper use of the law of value, and this accords with the essential requirement of the socialist system to feed and dress all the working people evenly and to make them equally well-off.

Otherwise, if we price mass consumption goods dear, we cannot reveal fully the excellence of the socialist system and possibly can cause inconveniences in the people's life. If, for example, the prices of fabrics—such as vynalon mixtures much demanded by our people—were set high, it would not be possible for all the people to dress decently. And if the prices of such school supplies as textbooks, pencils, notebooks and satchels were set high, children would not be properly educated despite the carrying out of compulsory education.

Nevertheless, there is a tendency among our functionaries to increase state budgetary revenue by raising without warrant the prices of fabrics and other mass consumption goods. As a result, though we turn out large quantities of fabrics, 20 meters per head of population, the working people cannot afford to buy enough to dress their children well as the prices are high. No doubt, the major reason why not enough cloth gets to the people is that our country still fails to turn out various fabrics at low costs. But it should be clearly borne in mind that the improper stance of the functionaries toward securing state budgetary revenue by means of raising the prices of cloth is also largely responsible for the small supply of cloth to the people. Owing to such erroneous acts of functionaries, the prices of fabrics have kept rising unreasonably over the past few years.

Unless our functionaries rectify such wrong ideas about attitudes to work, the people's conditions cannot be improved rapidly. In fact, it often happens that cloth does not sell because of excessive prices, remaining on the counter until, at last, it has to be sold out at reduced prices. This, in the end, not only will be harmful to the people's livelihood but render it impossible to secure the state budgetary revenue.

Our Party and government, therefore, assign low prices to mass consumption goods at least and, particularly, see to it that goods for children are priced so low that production costs are barely recovered, even if state budgetary revenue is not increased. This principle should be observed more extensively.

On the other hand, however, tobacco and drink, luxury goods, high-quality suit material and other wares which are in limited supply as yet, should be priced higher than mass consumption goods in order to adjust the demand for them. Charges for welfare facilities, including dwelling houses, should also be fixed on the same principle as the prices of commodities. Rents on ordinarily furnished one- or two-room flats, for example, should be cheap, but those on well-appointed dwellings with three or more rooms should be high because we do not have them in quantity. Of course, when our productive forces are developed high enough to assure all the goods and facilities needed by the people, it will become unnecessary to go to the trouble of taking such measures.

To fix the prices of commodities correctly, we must make them uniform. Unfair prices in some cases can be attributed to the failure by leading functionaries of the State Planning Commission, the Ministry of Finance and other economic agencies to exercise control over the fixing of prices on the goods produced by local industry enterprises, leaving it to the chairmen of the provincial people's committees on the plea that these goods are supposedly only of local significance. Therefore, just as the regional planning commissions have been set up to unify planning, regional price commissions should be established to unify the fixing of prices on goods, including those turned out by the local industry enterprises, and economic agencies such as the State Planning Commission, the Ministry of Finance and the Price Assessment Commisssion should strengthen their control over prices.

3. PROBLEMS OF THE PEASANT MARKET
AND ITS ABOLITION

The peasant market represents a form of trade whereby the peasants sell directly to the population, at definite places, part of the produce as well as animal products of the joint economy of cooperative farms, as well as products grown as a sideline by individual cooperative farmers. Though a form of trade in socialist society, the peasant market retains many remnants of capitalism. These are to be found in the fact that in the peasant market prices are determined spontaneously according to demand and supply and, therefore, the law of value operates somewhat blindly. The state does not plan demand and supply or prices for the peasant market. Of course, the spontaneous character of the peasant market undergoes certain restrictions as state trade develops and the coordinating function of the state over the peasant market grows. Yet, at the stage of socialism, the peasant market cannot completely be done away with.

The word *Jang* [market] originated neither under socialism nor capitalism; it is a term left over from feudal society. *Jang* came into being as handicrafts developed in the feudal age. From of old the Koreans call a merchant *Jang-sa-gun* which means "a person who does business at *Jang*." Thus, *Jang* is a backward form of trade that arose in feudal society. It is therefore preferable in principle that there be no peasant market, a backward form of trade, under the advanced, socialist system.

But, since the cooperative economy and individual sideline production both exist under socialism, the peasant market is inevitable, and it is not half bad that it exists. Some comrades seem to think that the state should purchase all the sideline products and market them in a planned way, but they are wrong, and it is not practicable either. As for the individual sideline products, the producers should be allowed to consume them, taking the surplus to the market to sell or barter for other goods according to their wish. As for the animal products and industrial crops turned out by the joint economy of cooperative farms, the greater part should be purchased by the state, but part should be divided among the peasants. They may consume them, sell them to the purchasing agents, or take them to the peasant market for sale. The peasants should not be forced to sell these products exclusively to the purchasing agents, but should be allowed to sell them to anybody they like, in this way making them more available to the people.

The textbook of political economy does not give a good account of the peasant market. It says only that the peasant market produces unfavorable effects on the development of the joint economy and fosters petty-bourgeois ideas and selfishness among the peasants. But no clear account is provided as to why the peasant market is necessary in socialist society, what role it plays and when it can be expected to disappear.

It is good rather than bad that sideline production and the peasant market still exist in socialist society. We are not yet in a position sufficiently to supply, through the channels of the state, all that is necessary for the people's life, above all, sundry goods for daily use like brooms and calabash-ladles, and subsidiary provisions like meat, eggs, gingili and wild sesame. Under the circumstances, what is wrong if individuals produce these things on the side and sell them in the market? Backward as it is, this way should still be utilized when advanced methods are not developed enough to cover everything.

Some functionaries fear that sideline production or the peasant market might revive capitalism right away. But there is no cause for such alarm. If the kitchen gardens given to cooperative farmers were too large, they might be engrossed in their individual farming, neglecting collective labor, and this might foster capitalist elements. But the kitchen gardens of our peasants are not bigger than a few dozen *pyong* each, and their individual sideline stockbreeding amounts to no more than raising a couple of pigs or a dozen or so chickens per household. Even if a peasant grows a few stalks of tobacco in his garden plot, it will not become capitalist management, and even if he takes a few chickens to the peasant market and sells them at somewhat higher prices, he will not become a capitalist.

But what would happen if the peasant market were abolished

by law on the supposed ground that sideline production as well as the peasant market had a harmful effect on the joint economy and fostered selfishness? The market place would disappear, of course, but the black market would remain. Peasants would knock at kitchen doors or hang about the back streets to sell chickens or eggs they raised on the side. Then they might be caught in this act, to be fined or punished otherwise by law. So forcible abolition of the peasant market would help find no solution, but rather might cause inconveniences to people and incriminate many senselessly.

Therefore, as long as the state cannot sufficiently produce and supply all the goods required by the people, we must guard strictly against the "Left" tendency to abolish the peasant market so hastily.

When, then, will individual sideline production and the peasant market disappear?

Firstly, they will disappear only when the country is industrialized, technology highly developed, and there is plenty of all the consumer goods people need. Nobody will trouble himself to go to the peasant market, when he can buy anything he wants from state-owned shops, and the peasant market will not deal in such goods either. Suppose cheap and good-quality chemical fibers gush forth in plenty from the factories. Then people will not take the trouble to go to the market place to buy the expensive cotton; and even if some peasants want to sell dear, such goods will not sell. Even under present circumstances, goods which are in plenty of supply are not sold in the peasant market; they are sold at uniform prices in all parts of our country, in big cities like Hamhung as well as in remote mountain villages like Potae-ri at the foot of Mt. Baekdu. When goods are plentiful and sold at uniform prices in this way, this amounts to a supply system.

It must be borne in mind, however, that goods which are in short supply are traded underhand or resold at the peasant market, even when uniform prices are fixed by the state. Some people buy goods from the shops and hoard them to sell them at higher prices when they are badly needed. Let me take the sale of eggs, for example. At present we produce eggs at the chicken farms built in Pyongyang and many other places. But we do not yet produce them to such an extent as to supply enough to the people. So there is a discrepancy between the state and the peasant-market price of eggs. To take advantage of this, the practice of reselling eggs has appeared.

Yet, we cannot, of course, send those who resell eggs to prison as criminals. As for other methods of control, there is no other way than taking some technical measures such as regulating the volume of sale per buyer. Of course, such measures should also be taken, but all they can accomplish is no more than to curb somewhat the concentration of goods in the hands of a few people. Such measures can by no means do away completely with reselling in the peasant market or black-marketeering.

To solve this problem large quantities of goods should be produced. If more egg farms are built and enough eggs are turned out to fully meet the needs of the people, the black-marketing of eggs will disappear, and buying and selling in the peasant market, too, will naturally come to an end. If the state meets the demands of the people in this way and eliminates from the peasant market, one by one, goods traded there, eventually the peasant market will no longer be needed.

Secondly, individual sideline production and the peasant market will cease to exist only when cooperative ownership is turned into ownership by the entire people.

As was pointed out in the "Theses on the Socialist Rural Question," there will be no more buying and selling in the peasant market when we have converted cooperative property into property of the entire people by organically merging the two forms of ownership, while steadily enhancing the leading role of property of the entire people over cooperative property.

One of the major reasons why the peasant market exists at present is that the cooperative and individual sideline economy exists side by side with the state economy.

Theefore, when the two kinds of ownership are welded into single ownership by the entire people the individual sideline economy will vanish, due to the developed productive forces, and, consequently, the peasant market will disappear and the circulation of commodities as a whole will become unnecessary. Then, products will be distributed under a supply system. At present, we distribute rice and some other indispensable goods to the workers and office employees under a supply system. Needless to say, this supply system was introduced not because the goods were abundant, nor was it introduced under the circumstances of single ownership by the entire people. We maintain the system with a view to assuring that people eat and live equally under circumstances where goods are not plenty. The system of supply we intend to introduce when the productive forces will be very highly developed and the two forms of property will be welded into a single property of the entire people, will be different from the one we have now. It will be a supply system aimed at providing the people more effectively with consumer goods turned out in large quantities, according to their diverse needs.

To conclude, the peasant market as well as underhand dealings will disappear and trade will go over finally to the supply system only when the productive forces have developed to such an extent that the state can turn out and supply in sufficient quantity all kinds of goods required by the people, and when cooperative ownership has grown into ownership of the entire people.

X.

GREAT RESULTS AND NEW PERSPECTIVES

THE FOURTH Congress of our Party* summed up the historic victory in building the foundations of socialism and adopted the magnificent program of the Seven-Year Plan. The main task set by the Plan was to achieve all-round technical reconstruction and cultural revolution and to improve radically the people's living standards as a result of the strengthening of the socialist system.

All our Party members and working people, with hope and confidence in a bright future, successfully carried the grand Seven-Year Plan into effect, accomplishing fresh innovations and miracles every day.

However, over the past few years our revolution and construction were faced with great difficulties and hardships as the aggressive maneuvers of the U.S. imperialists became more threatening and as a complicated situation was brought about in the international communist movement. This urgently required our Party to arm the entire people firmly with the revolutionary ideas of Marxism-Leninism and, especially, to make thorough-going politico-ideological preparations for coping with war. At the same time, great efforts were required to strengthen the nation's defense power—even if it meant some readjustment of the tempo of development of the national economy—to safeguard fully the security of the country and the people.

*See Chapter II.

From *Report on the Work of the Central Committee to the Fifth Congress of the Workers Party of Korea.* November 2, 1970.

The Party held a historic Conference in October 1966*, where it took solid steps to strengthen our revolutionary ranks politically and ideologically and to reorganize entirely the work of socialist construction in conformity with the requirements of the prevailing situation. It advanced a new revolutionary line of simultaneously carrying on economic construction and defense preparations to increase the nation's capabilities for meeting the intensified aggressive maneuvers of the enemy and, accordingly, decided to put off the fulfillment of the Seven-Year Plan for three years.

The ensuing developments have clearly shown that the steps taken by the Party were in full accord with the fundamental interests of our revolution and that they were daring, dynamic and wise measures for meeting the changing situation. All our Party members and working people, true to the new revolutionary line advanced by the Party, have waged a heroic fight on the two fronts of economic construction and defense, and fulfilled the Seven-Year Plan creditably, achieving stalwart politico-ideological unity throughout our society and making the whole country into a strong fortress capable of resisting any surprise invasion by the enemy.

CONVERSION INTO A SOCIALIST INDUSTRIAL STATE

The greatest achievement in socialist construction during the period under review** is that our country has been converted into a socialist industrial state as a result of the splendid fulfillment of the historic task of socialist industrialization.

Socialist industrialization was a matter of pressing urgency in reinforcing the established socialist system and advancing socialist construction in the northern half of the Republic, the cardinal task of the Seven-Year Plan.

Relying on the foundations of an independent national industry and the material basis for equipping all branches of the national

*See Chapter VI
**The period since the Fourth Party Congress, 1961.

economy with up-to-date technology already prepared in the period of the Five-Year Plan, our Party saw to it that a powerful effort was unfolded in the Seven-Year Plan period to build an independent modern industry—comprehensively developed, possessed of a solid raw-material base of its own, and equipped with new techniques—and to effect the all-round technical reconstruction of the national economy.

In accordance with the correct policy of the Party, industry developed very rapidly and its look changed radically during the Seven-Year Plan.

Thanks to the successful carrying out of the Seven-Year Plan in the field of industry, this year [1970] the value of gross industrial output will increase 11.6 times as against 1956—13.3 times in the production of the means of production and 9.3 times in consumer goods. This means that industrial production grew at a high rate of 19.1 per cent on an annual average over the whole period of industrialization, from 1957 to 1970. Today our industry makes in only 12 days as much as was turned out in the entire pre-Liberation year of 1944.

Industry as a whole has developed at a high rate and heavy industry particularly has advanced very rapidly. In the Seven-Year Plan period our Party saw to it that emphasis was laid primarily on the work of improving and reinforcing the key branches of heavy industry, at the same time carrying out extensive work to expand and consolidate the bases for heavy industry. As a result of the implementation of the Party's policy our heavy industry was fully equipped with its own powerful machine-building industry as the core, and its might increased greatly during the period under review.

The biggest success in the building of heavy industry is the establishment of our own machine-building industry, the basis for the development of the national economy and technical progress.

Thanks to the great efforts directed by the Party to the development of the machine-building industry in the Seven-Year Plan period, our country, which could not make even simple farm implements properly before the Liberation, is now in a position to manufacture large-scale machines, such as 6,000-ton presses, heavy-duty lorries, large tractors, excavators and bulldozers, electric and diesel locomotives, and vessels of the 5,000-ton class, as well as precision machines, and to produce not only separate units of equipment but supply complete plants for modern factories. In the Seven-Year Plan period alone, our engineering industry has produced and supplied aggregate plants for more than 100 modern units, such as power stations and metallurgical and chemical factories.

The power bases of the country, too, have been further consolidated to meet the demands of rapid industrial development and all-round technical revolution. Giant hydro- and thermo-power plants were built during the Seven-Year Plan, with the result that the total generating capacity of our country has grown markedly; the one-sidedness of the power industry which had relied exclusively upon hydraulic power has been eliminated and the nation's power bases improved qualitatively.

Rapid development of the ferrous metallurgical industry was one of the important tasks in realizing overall industrialization. In the Seven-Year Plan period the existing iron-producing bases were expanded and a new iron works was built in the western region, with the result that the pig and granulated iron production capacity has increased and the independence of the iron industry strengthened; production of steel, rolled steel in particular, made rapid progress and a number of second-stage metal-processing branches have been newly founded. The ferrous metallurgical industry of our country has now grown into a powerful industrial domain equipped with perfect production processes—from the production of pig iron to the production of steel, rolled steel and goods of second-stage metal processing—and it fills demands for various kinds of metals needed for the development of the national economy.

The look of the chemical industry has also changed fundamentally. During the period of industrialization the bases of chemical-fertilizer production were reinforced and a new branch producing agricultural chemicals and branches producing vynalon and other synthetic fibers and resins came into being, with the result that powerful bases of the organic as well as the inorganic chemical industry have been laid in our country, rendering it possible to accelerate chemicalization more vigorously.

Rapid progress has also been made in the coal, ore-mining and building-materials industries and in other branches of heavy industry.

This year our heavy industry will turn out 16 billion kwh of electricity, 27 million tons of coal, 2 million tons of steel, 1.5 million tons of chemical fertilizers and 4 million tons of cement.

Our heavy industry, with the powerful machine-building industry as its core, reliably guarantees the political and economic independence of the country. As the solid material foundation for the faster development of the national economy, it displays great strength in developing light industry and the rural economy, while augmenting the nation's defense power.

Epochal headway has been made in the development of light industry, too. The Party firmly maintained the policy of developing large-scale central industries and, simultaneously, medium- and small-scale local industries in the production of popular consumption goods. During the Seven-Year Plan period new up-to-date central factories of light industry were set up and, at the same time, many local-industry factories were built with locally available reserves; the technical reconstruction of local industry was pushed ahead actively in keeping with the development of heavy industry. As a result, our country now has all branches of light industrial production, including a textile industry capable of turning out more than 400 million meters of high-quality fabrics a year, a foodstuff industry and industry capable of turning out daily necessities. There have been established up-to-date light-industry bases which can meet by their own production the demands of the working people for consumer goods, ranging from drapery to cultural products.

As it advanced at a rapid speed and its size expanded, industry came to play a more decisive role in gross social production and in the national income. The share of industry in the total industrial and agricultural output, by value, rose from 34 per cent in 1956 to 74 per cent in 1969, and the share of industry in the national income increased from 25 to 65 per cent in the same period.

Further, there has been a marked rise in the per capita output of major manufactured goods, an important index to the economic might and level of industrial development of a nation. This year the per capita output of our country will be 1,184 kwh in electricity, 1,975 kilograms in coal, 158 kilograms in steel, 108 kilograms in chemical fertilizers, and 287 kilograms in cement. This shows that our country has reached the level of advanced industrial countries in the per capita output of major industrial products and even surpassed them in some items.

The overall technical revolution has also been carried to success in every field of the national economy, thanks to the powerful heavy-industry bases of our own. With the development of the machine-building industry and other heavy industries, technical equipment has been improved fundamentally in all domains of the national economy, and electrification and automation applied extensively.

Technical reconstruction of the rural economy has been realized successfully with the powerful support of heavy industry.

The Party has directed great efforts to the technical reorganization of the rural economy in keeping with the policy put forth at its Fourth Congress and, particularly, along the path illumined by the "Theses on the Socialist Rural Question in Our Country" adopted at the Eighth Plenary Meeting of the Fourth Central Committee of the Party in 1964,* and has brought about brilliant successes in this field.

The greatest success gained in the rural technical revolution during the period under review is the completion of irrigation.

We carried on irrigation works on a large scale while effectively utilizing the existing irrigation facilities, thereby completing the irrigation of paddy fields and effecting even the irrigation of dry fields significantly. Also, great efforts were made by the state to carry out draining projects in the past few years, with the result

*See Chapter III.

that major rice-producing areas are now completely free from the damage of standing water. River improvement projects, dykes for controlling tidewater, and afforestation works were undertaken extensively in all parts of the country; paddy and dry fields as well as crops were better protected against natural calamities. Consequently, during the period under review there has been established in our country a reliable system of irrigation that always ensures rich and stable harvests against drought or flood.

The Party posed mechanization as the central task in the rural technical revolution during the Seven-Year Plan and fought energetically to carry it out. During the period under review, the number of farm-machine stations, the basis of rural mechanization, increased considerably; they were set up in every city and county of our country and many up-to-date farm machines were supplied to the countryside. The number of tractors serving the rural economy grew 3.3 times, and lorries 6.4 times in the period from 1961 to 1969, and various kinds of new farm machines were invented and manufactured, so that more farm work could be done by machines.

The task of electrification in the countryside has also been performed with credit during the Seven-Year Plan. A struggle was mounted to supply every *ri* and farmhouse with electricity. As a result, every *ri* now has electricity and every farm household electric lights. In the countryside, electricity is used widely not only in the home life of peasants but as power for machines and as a heat source in agricultural production. At present, the annual consumption of electricity in the countryside amounts to one billion kwh, which is used mostly in production. The proportion of electricity consumed in the countryside is very great, and our country has already attained the level of the world's advanced countries in the field of rural electrification.

Great progress has been registered in the chemicalization of agriculture as well. The amount of chemical fertilizers applied per *chongbo* of paddy and dry fields last year was 3.2 times more than in 1960 and their qualitative composition was also greatly improved. Besides, with an increased amount of agricultural chemicals sprayed, crops were protected more efficiently against damage from blights and insect pests; the countryside was supplied with a considerable amount of highly effective herbicides.

All branches of agricultural production advanced apace as the rural technical revolution progressed successfully.

Despite certain fluctuations in agricultural production caused by the unusually severe natural calamities which hit our country over the past few years, we reaped a good harvest every year, and this year, too, have gathered in a big bumper crop. In our country, the food problem has now been solved completely and there has been laid the firm basis of grain production which will make it possible to develop all other domains of the rural economy more speedily. With the solid material and technical foundations laid for stockbreeding, animal husbandry has entered a new path of development on the basis of up-to-date technology. Especially, has there been a great turn in the development of the poultry industry in the past few years, and now we can produce over 700 million eggs and large quantities of chickens every year by industrial methods.

The electrification of railways is one of the major achievements in the technical reconstruction of the national economy. During the Seven-Year Plan the 850-kilometer railway sections have newly been electrified and the electrification of the major trunk lines has been completed in the main.

All this shows that the historic task of socialist industrialization in our country has been carried out splendidly and our land, once a colonial agrarian country far removed from modern technical civilization, has turned into a socialist industrial state possessed of a modern industry and developed agriculture.

The course of the implementation of the Party's line of industrialization was by no means a royal road; there were not a few obstacles and hardships that had to be overcome by our people to build a modern industry and carry into effect the technical reconstruction of the national economy.

We took over a negligible colonial industry from the old society and even that was destroyed severely in the war instigated by the U.S. imperialist aggressors. During the postwar Three-Year Plan the task of rehabilitation and reconstruction of the war-ravaged national economy was fulfilled with success, but the colonial lopsidedness of industry was not fully eradicated and the foundations of heavy industry were extremely weak. We had limited funds, insufficient raw and other materials, and small technical resources. Moreover, we had to wage a struggle to realize industrialization and the technical reconstruction of the national economy in the very complicated internal and external conditions of our revolution, especially in the strained circumstances in which the U.S. imperialists occupying South Korea and their stooges ceaselessly intensified their maneuvers to provoke war.

The Party, however, carried forward the line of socialist industrialization without the slightest vacillation and, inspiring our people with the revolutionary spirit of self-reliance, showed them how to solve with their own efforts all the difficult and intricate problems of building a modern industry and realizing the technical reconstruction of the national economy.

All the working people of our country, upholding the Party's line, unanimously rallied to the struggle for the socialist industrialization of the country and technical reconstruction. In response to the Party's call—"Let us dash forward at the speed of Chollima!"—our heroic working class and all working people waged an indefatigable fight to implement the Party's line of industrialization, smashing passivism and conservatism standing in the way of their advance and surmounting all hardships and difficulties.

Thanks to the Party's correct line of industrialization, its wise guidance in the implementation of the line, and to the heroic and devoted labor struggle of our people, the difficult and complex task of industrialization, which took capitalist countries a full century and even a few centuries, has been creditably accomplished in our country in the very short period of only 14 years.

The conversion into a socialist industrial state—this is a great event of historic significance in the struggle to step up the building of socialism and communism in our country and attain a nationwide victory for the Korean revolution.

As a result of socialist industrialization, our country has been provided with the firm material and technical foundations of socialism and has become fully axle to satisfy from its own production the demands of economic construction and defense as well as the living needs of the people. The conversion of our country into an industrial state has made our revolutionary base impregnable and provided solid ground for strong support to the revolutionary struggle of the South Korean people, the unification of the fatherland, and its future prosperity.

With the founding of an independent modern industry and the equipping of all domains of the national economy, including agriculture, with modern techniques, our country finally has done away with its economic and technical backwardness, the vestige of the old society, and joined the ranks of advanced countries of the world as a full-fledged member. Our people, freed forever from former subjection to all sorts of humiliation and contempt for their backward economy, is now able to enter the international arena with pride as a mighty and advanced nation on a par with all the big and small nations of the world.

NEW TASKS OF SOCIALIST
ECONOMIC CONSTRUCTION

During the Seven-Year Plan we have founded a self-supporting modern industry and put all branches of the national economy basically on the foundation of up-to-date technology by vigorously accelerating the socialist industrialization of the country and the all-round technical reconstruction of the national economy.

However, we still have much work to do in the field of economic construction if we are to lay the solid material and technical foundations for socialism. We should equip industry even better and strengthen its independence, bringing its potential into full play in our country, and develop the nation's productive forces still faster by assuring steady technical progress in all fields of the national economy.

The basic task of the Six-Year Plan in the field of socialist economic construction is to further cement the material and technical foundations of socialism and free the working people from arduous labor in all fields of the national economy, by consolidating and carrying forward the successes gained in industrialization and advancing the technical revolution to a new, higher plane.

During the period of the new prospective plan we should, above all, perfect the infra-structures of the industrial branches and strengthen the *Juche* character of our industry still further.

With socialist industrialization, our industry not only has attained a well-balanced structure and equipped itself with new techniques, but for the most part it also has developed on the basis of domestic raw material resources, and has an enormous potential. Our industry, however, does not yet employ its full potential since some of its branches have not yet been perfected and minor and secondary sections and production processes have not been put into proper shape. We still depend on foreign countries for some raw materials, which cannot but affect the secure and normal development of our industry to a certain degree.

We should continue with the work of rounding out all branches of industry to reinforce weak sections and create those branches we need to perfect our industry quickly. At the same time, we should wage a dynamic struggle to develop industry entirely on the basis of raw materials available in our country. We should in this way bring the power of our industry into full play and base all industrial branches on *Juche* so firmly that they will be at least 60 to 70 per cent self-reliant with regard to raw materials.

It is important vigorously to push ahead with the technical revolution to liberate the working people from arduous labor. The technical revolution is also a very urgent problem in easing the present shortage of labor.

We have relieved our working people of heavy and laborious work in no small measure by stepping up technical reconstruction on a full scale in all fields of the national economy during the Seven-Year Plan. But distinctions between heavy and light labor still remain, and heat-affected and harmful labor have not yet been eliminated in our country. There is a big disparity between industrial and agricultural labor; the women, who account for one half of the population, have not yet been freed from household burdens completely.

We should unfold an extensive technical innovation movement in industry and agriculture and all other branches of the national economy to narrow the distinctions between heavy and light labor and between agricultural and industrial work to a considerable extent, and to free the women from the heavy burden of household chores. These are precisely the three major tasks of the technical revolution we should fulfill in the next few years.

Great efforts should be exerted, first of all, to reduce the difference between heavy and light labor, eliminate heat-affected and harmful labor, and widely to introduce semi-automation in all fields of the national economy.

The first and foremost task here is to unfold a widespread technical innovation movement in the mining industry where hard and labor-consuming work exists more than in any other branches, to make labor in this field easy, highly productive and safer.

The ore mines and bituminous coal mines should effect comprehensive mechanization and gradually go over to semi-automation and automation. A decisive upswing should be brought about in mechanization at the anthracite mines, which account for an overwhelming proportion in the coal output of our country, and where the level of mechanization of work is low.

The level of mechanization should generally be raised in the realm of forestry. The fishing industry should equip itself with large, modern and all-purpose vessels to realize comprehensive mechanization.

Capital construction, along with the mining industry, is a domain where heavy labor still prevails. Efficient building machines should be supplied in greater numbers and the proportion of precast construction raised further to raise the level of mechanization decisively in this field.

Mechanization of loading and unloading operations is one of the important ways to eliminate heavy labor. Such operations have not yet been fully mechanized at railway stations, wharves, construction sites and in various other branches of the national economy. Hence, not only are quite a few people still engaged in heavy work but, also, rapidity of operations is not assured. This is one of the reasons for our failure to increase the utilization of the means of transportation. During the period of the new prospective plan we should manufacture and supply various types of efficient loading and unloading equipment in large quantities to speed up the mechanization of these operations.

A technical innovation movement should be unfolded in industry to do away with heat-affected and harmful labor.

Production processes should be automated to eliminate heat-affected labor once and for all in the ferrous metallurgical, chemical and cement industries and in other domains where work is done under high temperatures. We should automate all production processes which involve heat-affected labor, beginning with those branches where the heat is particularly intense, and go over to remote control step by step.

The health of workers, as well as production itself is still affected to a certain extent by gas, dust and other noxious matters emitted by processes used in the chemical, non-ferrous metallurgical, mining and building materials industries, and in a number of other domains. We should facilitate technical reconstruction in these branches of production to do away with harmful labor as soon as possible.

We should, in this way, convert harmful labor into harmless labor and thoroughly prevent the health of workers, as well as production, from being affected by heat, gas, dust and humidity in all industrial branches and work places.

Promotion of the rural technical revolution is a very pressing task before us today. We should carry out the all-round mechanization and chemicalization of agriculture in the Six-Year Plan period to narrow down drastically the distinctions between agricultural and industrial labor, and to save much labor in the countryside.

We should make more effective use of the existing farm

machines, and manufacture in greater quantities various types of modern farm machines, particularly, efficient machines suited to the topographical conditions of our country, to put widely into effect the comprehensive mechanization of agriculture. In the period of the new prospective plan an all-people movement should be waged to introduce comprehensive mechanization, first in the two-crop dry fields under irrigation and in the paddy fields where rice is sown directly, and gradually expand its applications to realize comprehensive, all-round mechanization of agriculture in the near future.

Extensive readjustment of land is an urgent task in realizing the all-round mechanization of agriculture. It is mainly because the land is not readjusted properly that we have failed to push forward the mechanization of agriculture at a rapid pace, although we now have a considerable number of tractors, lorries and up-to-date farm machines of various types. Land readjustment should be launched in a movement of the masses to enlarge and trim the plots and terrace the slopes so that machines may work effectively in both paddy and non-paddy fields.

Machines alone cannot replace all manual labor in the rural economy and, accordingly, farm work which cannot be performed by machines should be done with the aid of chemistry. Weeding, a most painstaking and labor-consuming work, should be done by chemical methods in a wide application of various highly efficient herbicides.

By bringing about a big advance in the rural technical revolution we should in the near future reduce the labor force expended per *chongbo* of paddies to 60-80 man-days and that of dry fields to 20-30 man-days on an average, thus enabling a farmer to cultivate five to six *chongbo* of paddies or eight to ten *chongbo* of dry fields at least. An eight-hour working day should thus gradually be introduced in the cooperative farms, as in the factories and enterprises, and the difference between town and country in working conditions should be lessened significantly.

One of the important tasks we should fulfill is to carry out a technical revolution to free women from the burdens of kitchen and household work. Our Party has not only accomplished the social emancipation of women but has also made untiring efforts to provide better conditions for them to participate in broad areas of public life. With the deep solicitude of the Party, our women are now making positive contributions to revolutionary struggle and constructive work as proud masters of the country.

But today our women still have to devote much time to household work while they are engaged in public activities side by side with men. Accordingly, they are under the double burden of public activities and domestic affairs. We should give deep attention to technical innovations required to extricate women from household chores and further enhance their role in the revolution and construction.

Most important in lightening the kitchen work of women is to bring about fresh innovations in the foodstuff industry. The processing of various kinds of subsidiary and staple foods should be developed extensively so that all foodstuffs may be processed by industrial methods and supplied locally for the preparation of food quickly and easily at home.

While developing the foodstuff industry, we must produce and supply a large quantity of domestic refrigerators, washing machines, electric cooking pots and various other kitchen utensil, so that women need not spend much time in kitchen work and household chores.

When all these tasks of the technical revolution are fulfilled with success, all the working people of our country will be freed from toilsome, labor-consuming and inefficient work and attain high labor productivity, while doing their work safely and easily, and their life will become more affluent.

SOCIALIST CULTURAL DEVELOPMENT

Socialism and communism require not only a high level of development of the productive forces but a high cultural standard of the working people. Only when the cultural revolution, along with the technical revolution, is pushed ahead continuously and vigorously, can the complete victory of socialism be hastened and the essential requirements of socialist and communist society be satisfied.

One of the most important tasks in the building of socialist national culture at present is to struggle against cultural infiltration by imperialism.

It is a law-given requirement of the building of socialist national culture to fight against the outmoded culture of the exploiter society and reactionary capitalist culture. Especially, under present circumstances when the imperialists are conspiring to spread reactionary bourgeois culture among us, is it very urgent to combat all sorts of reactionary cultural trends.

Cultural infiltration, one of the principal methods employed by the imperialists in the execution of their neo-colonialist policy, serves their policy of foreign aggression. The imperialists, led by U.S. imperialism, craftily seek to obliterate the national culture of other countries, paralyze the people's consciousness of national independence and their revolutionary spirit, and demoralize and degenerate the people through cultural infiltration. One of the salient examples is the ideological and cultural infiltration by the U.S. imperialists and the Japanese militarists into South Korea. Due to the policy of obliterating national culture pursued by the U.S. and Japanese reactionaries and their stooges, in South Korea at present our national culture is wantonly trampled underfoot and corrupt "Yankee culture," Japanese fashions and the Japanese way of life hold sway, corroding the spiritual life of the people. The U.S. imperialists seek maliciously to infiltrate their reactionary culture not only into South Korea but also into the northern half of the Republic, and employ every conceivable means, such as broadcasts, the press, and literary and art works.

Unless such imperialist cultural infiltration is effectively checked socialist national culture cannot be developed on a sound basis nor can socialist gains firmly be defended. Historical experience shows that if imperialist cultural infiltration is not checked decisively, if the reactionary bourgeois elements are tolerated even to the slightest degree in the domain of culture, the national culture will gradually wear away, the people will harbor illusions in imperialism, and suffer from ideological disorders; further, the revolution and construction will encounter grave difficulties and crises.

We must, therefore, direct the spearhead of the cultural revolution, first of all, against cultural infiltration by the imperialists. We should strictly guard against infiltration into our ranks of all varieties of rotten bourgeois culture or life styles, and should never tolerate bourgeois elements, however trivial, in the realm of cultural development.

For the sound development of socialist national culture, it is also necessary resolutely to oppose the trend of restorationism.

Restorationism is an anti-Marxist ideological trend which restores and glorifies the things of the past uncritically, in disregard of the demands of the times and the class principle. If restorationism is allowed in the field of cultural development, all the unsound aspects of the culture of the past will be revived, and reactionary bourgeois and feudalistic Confucian ideas, as well as other outmoded ideas, will grow in the minds of the people.

A relentless struggle should be waged against the tendency to copy blindly the antiquated, reactionary things of the past, idealizing and embellishing them on the pretext of taking over the heritage of national culture. We must discard backward and reactionary elements in the cultural heritage, and critically inherit and develop progressive and popular elements in conformity with the realities of socialism today.

We must unfold a vigorous ideological battle in the domain of culture to prevent imperialist cultural infiltration and overcome the tendency of restorationism, thereby more rapidly developing all branches of socialist culture on a wholesome basis, including education, science, literature and art.

The most important task in the field of education is to build up a large contingent of technicians and specialists, of intellectuals, in our country.

Today the productive forces have reached a very high stage of development and the scale of the economy has also grown incomparably. Unless we train more technicians and specialists, we cannot run properly the national economy equipped with up-to-date techniques, nor can we fulfill the tasks of the technical revolution now confronting us.

We must train technicians and specialists on a large scale to meet the practical demands of socialist construction, so that the number of engineers, assistant engineers and specialists graduated from colleges and higher technical schools accounts for more than 10 per cent of the labor force at all factories, enterprises and cooperative farms during the period of the new prospective plan. The number of technicians and specialists should exceed one million in the near future.*

To train a large number of technicians and specialists the existing colleges and higher technical schools should be improved and strengthened, the scope of training widened, and more new colleges set up at the center and in the provinces according to the calculated demand of each branch of the national economy for technical personnel. Also, the number of factory colleges and factory higher technical schools should be greatly increased, education at night schools and correspondence courses further improved.

Along with the training of a large army of intellectuals, we must continue energetically to raise the level of the general and technical knowledge of working people.

At present the entire rising generation receives technical schooling before going out into the world as a result of the introduction of universal, compulsory nine-year technical education.** To raise the general cultural and technical levels of the working people it is therefore important to improve the quality of compulsory technical schooling. The ranks of teachers should be increased, and the contents and methods of education improved constantly.

---

*Between 1960 and 1970, as reported by Kim Il Sung at the Fifth Party Congress, the number of universities and colleges increased from 78 to 129, and 376 new higher technical schools were established. By 1970, there were more than 497,000 engineers and specialists, or four times the number in 1960.
**Established in 1967 for ages 8 to 17.

To achieve our objective in this field we must also continue to raise the technical and cultural level of adults who were denied the opportunity of learning in the exploiter society of the past. We must see to it that all working people study regularly under definite educational systems.

Press circulation and radio broadcasting should be improved. Especially, the telecasting network should be extended to cover the entire country in the near future.

We should continue to develop the work of bringing up children under state and public care, an essential task for the cultural revolution and the building of socialist society.

It is an important communist policy and method of education to rear children under public care. A person's character and thinking are evolved from childhood; accordingly, proper education and cultivation of good habits in the early years exert strong influence on future development. The public upbringing of children accustoms them to organized and disciplined life, fosters the spirit of collectivism and communist character, getting them used to the style of organizational life from childhood.

We must enlarge accommodations at existing creches and kindergartens and erect many more modern ones so that excellent facilities for the education of children may be provided at all places where there are children. Thus we must see to it that all preschool children of our country are brought up at creches and kindergartens, at state and public expense.

Today the gigantic tasks of socialist construction, especially the new technical revolution, demand the decisive advance of scientific research. In the sphere of natural science, main efforts should be directed to the solution of scientific and technological problems related to the more effective use of the economic foundations already laid, the further strengthening of the *Juche* character of our industry and the development of the technical revolution to a higher level, while new scientific and technological domains actively should be explored. In the field of social science, it is necessary theoretically to generalize the achievements and rich experience gained by our people in revolutionary struggle and construction work, and demonstrate the correctness of our Party's line and policies with more profundity.

Literature and art assume a major role in the communist education of the working people and in the revolutionization and "working-classization" of the whole of society.

The important task in this realm is to create more revolutionary works dedicated to arming the working people with the communist world outlook. Writers and artists should create more works on the themes of the glorious revolutionary traditions, the deep roots of our Party and revolution, the heroic feats of the valiant People's Armymen and the people who, carrying forward the brilliant revolutionary traditions of the anti-Japanese armed struggle, fought bravely during the Fatherland Liberation War. At the same time, they should give a vivid portrayal of the grand reality of today in which our people are seething with revolutionary zeal, dashing forward like a hurricane in the saddle of Chollima, and of their worthwhile life. They should adequately present the revolutionary struggle of the South Korean revolutionaries and patriots who are fighting valiantly for the South Korean revolution and for the unification of the fatherland. Writers and artists should go deeper into reality, seriously delve into life, employing the creative methods of socialist realism to produce many revolutionary works that will pull at people's heartstrings and encourage and inspire them in their progress.

The masses of the people are the makers of socialist culture; literature and art in our society can advance speedily only with the wide participation of the working masses. We must guard strictly against the tendency toward professionalism in literary and art activities, smash mysticism in creative work, and develop literature and art on a broad mass scale.

Language is one of the common features of a nation, a powerful weapon for scientific and technological advance, a major index that characterizes the national form of culture. Therefore, socialist national culture can hardly be built successfully without developing national language.

Our language, which is a priceless national treasure of our

people and a national pride, is undergoing a grave crisis in South Korea today. Owing to the U.S. imperialists' policy of blotting out the national language, our language is gradually losing its purity and deteriorating into a polyglot language in South Korea. This arouses serious concern among our people. We must unfold a vigorous nationwide movement to protect our language from obliteration by U.S. imperialism and its stooges, for the brilliant development and flowering of socialist national culture and for the everlasting prosperity of our nation. At the same time, we must strive energetically to make active use of pure native words and develop their use in conformity to present-day requirements.

Good physique of the working people constitutes the basis for the revolutionary struggle and the building of a wealthy and mighty society. We must popularize physical culture and sports an extensively develop physical training for national defense so as to promote the physical strength of all working people and firmly prepare the entire people for labor and national defense. We must thoroughly establish *Juche* in physical culture and sports and rapidly develop athletic science and techniques.

By successfully carrying out all these tasks of the cultural revolution we must make our culture a true people's culture which serves the socialist working people, a militant and revolutionary culture which contributes positively to the revolutionary struggle and construction.

THE IDEOLOGICAL REVOLUTION

The ideological revolution is an acute class struggle to liquidate capitalism forever even in the realm of man's consciousness and to carry forward the important revolutionary task of completely freeing all working people from the fetters of obsolete ideologies, arming them with progressive working-class ideas, the ideas of communism. To carry out the ideological revolution thoroughly means to carry the revolution itself through to the end; accordingly, this is one of the fundamental questions determining success in building socialism and communism. A Marxist-

Leninist Party which has seized power can assure the victory of the revolutionary cause of the working class only when it repudiates all deviations that may arise in this domain and solves the problem correctly. Historical experience shows that if a Marxist-Leninist Party does not steadily encourage the class awakening of the popular masses and strengthen the ideological revolution among them, the influence of bourgeois ideas will increase, paralyzing the revolutionary consciousness of the working people, with the consequence that the socialist system can then hardly be consolidated and developed, and even the gains of the revolution already won can be jeopardized. On the consistent line of the Party we must continue energetically to drive forward the ideological revolution and give it definite priority in all work.

To realize the "working-classizing" of the whole of society while strenuously pursuing the course of revolutionizing all working people by giving priority to the ideological revolution— this is a weighty task that must be fulfilled without fail in the period of transition from capitalism to socialism. Only by "working-classizing" all the members of society, is it possible to obliterate class distinctions, build a classless society and win complete victory for socialism. However, even after the whole of society has been "working-classized" and the tasks of the period of transition from capitalism to socialism carried out successfully, the survivals of outworn ideologies will not be eradicated completely from the minds of people, and therefore it cannot be said that all working people will have become real Communists. Even after the complete victory of socialism the Marxist-Leninist Party should continue the struggle to revolutionize and "working-classize" all working people. Only in this way can the ideological fortress of communism be solidly built.

During the period under review we have vigorously pursued the Party's line of revolutionizing and "working-classizing" the whole of society, and registered no little success in this field. This is no more than an initial achievement, however. We have just started. We should further deepen and develop this work on the basis of the successes and experience gained in the past period.

First of all, communist education should be further intensified among the working people. In this respect, what is fundamental is class education. There can be no communist ideas apart from the revolutionary ideas of the working class; there can be no communist education apart from class education. The class consciousness of the working class forms the kernel of communist ideology. Therefore, only when the working people are firmly armed with working-class consciousness can they become real Communists. We should equip all working people with the working-class viewpoint so that they will hate the class enemies and fight relentlessly against imperialism and the exploiting system. Particularly, we should deepen the hatred of the working people for U.S. imperialism and Japanese militarism, the main targets of our struggle, and firmly prepare the entire people ideologically so that they may fight staunchly at any time to force the U.S. imperialists out of South Korea and carry the revolutionary cause of national unification through to the end.

Collectivism is intrinsically the basic characteristic of the working class. It is the foundation of life in socialist and communist society where the working people are closely united and strive to attain the common goal. We should keep paying profound attention to strengthening the education of the working people in collectivism. To equip people with the ideas of collectivism an intensified struggle should be waged against individualism and egoism, above all. Education should be conducted among the working people to cultivate the revolutionary spirit of love for the collective and organization, and of working with devotion at any time and place for the benefit of society and the people, for the benefit of the Party and the revolution, instead of seeking personal ease and comfort, so that all will work, study and live in the communist spirit of "One for all and all for one."

Fostering a communist attitude toward labor holds an important place in communist education. We should educate the working people to love labor, regard it as a most honorable thing, display voluntary enthusiasm and creativity in their work, and sincerely participate in communal labor for the collective and society.

Education in socialist patriotism should also be emphasized. Socialist patriotism means love for the socialist fatherland—the proletarian dictatorship, the socialist system and the independent national economy, which are the gains of our revolution. Only when the working people are firmly armed with the idea of socialist patriotism, can they resolutely fight for the prosperity and progress of the fatherland and for the victory of the revolution. We should convince all working people clearly of the revolutionary essence of the proletarian dictatorship, the true superiority of the socialist system and the might of the independent national economy so that they feel great pride and glory in living in the socialist fatherland and infinitely treasure the socialist gains won and secured by our people at the cost of their blood and sweat, and strive actively for their consolidation and development. We should patiently educate all working people to value and protect the property of the country and the people, with the attitude of a master toward the nation's economic life, and strive with all their wisdom, talent and energy to make greater contributions to the building of a socialist fatherland, rich and strong.

Communist education of the working people must necessarily be conducted in close combination with education in revolutionary traditions.

Our revolutionary traditions were established in the course of creatively developing Marxist-Leninist theory to suit the specific conditions of the Korean revolution, thoroughly combining revolutionary theories and revolutionary practice; they are priceless revolutionary wealth obtained amid the flames of the unprecedentedly arduous and sanguinary anti-Japanese armed struggle. Experience shows that communist education, when linked up with education in revolutionary traditions, has a vital influence and moves people profoundly. Education in revolutionary traditions is necessary for everyone, and it is all the more essential particularly for the younger generation which has not undergone the ordeals of revolutionary struggle. Revolution continues and one generation is replaced by another. Only when the rising generation is educated in revolutionary traditions will it be possible to rear its members as genuine continuators of our revolution, to carry on the revolution through the generations.

We should fully acquaint the working people with the historical roots of our Party and our revolution, thoroughly transmitting to them the infinite fidelity of the revolutionary forerunners to the revolutionary cause and their indefatigable fighting will and revolutionary optimism. At the same time, the working people should be equipped with the experience in revolutionary struggle and the communist method and style of work acquired during the period of the anti-Japanese armed struggle.

Our Party's line and policies are a creative application and development of the universal principles of Marxism-Leninism to suit the specific realities of our country. They are the most effective strategies and tactics for the successful accomplishment of our revolution and a guide to all our actions. Only when the Party members and working people are firmly armed with our Party's revolutionary ideas can they become true revolutionaries, loyal to the Party and the revolution, and properly carry out the revolutionary tasks assigned to them. We ought to intensify even more the education of Party members and the working people in the policies of the Party so that they may clearly understand the quintessence and correctness of the Party's policies and make them their unshakable faith. In this way, we must see that everyone works in strict adherence to the Party's policies at any time and place, and fights resolutely to defend and carry them through to the end in any adversity, by firmly arming himself with the unitary ideology of our Party and making the Party's line and policies his bones and flesh.

Revolutionary practice is a powerful means for remolding the ideological consciousness of people. People are tempered constantly and made into revolutionaries in the course of the arduous and complex practical struggle to remake nature and society. We should link the ideological work of educating and remolding the working people with the revolutionary struggle and practical activities in the building of socialism and communism, so that they may steel themselves ideologically and cultivate a strong revolutionary will in the course of performing their revolutionary tasks. Particularly, the intellectuals, who are disconnected from practical productive activities, should at all times be made to go deep into the midst of practical socialist construction to round out their knowledge acquired from books, and discover new scientific and technical problems, while also learning from the organization and militancy of the working class and its allegiance to the Party and the revolution.

One of the essential means for revolutionizing and "working-classizing" people is to strengthen their revolutionary organizational life.

A major criterion of the Communist is strong revolutionary organization. Only he who is possessed of a strong sense of revolutionary organization, as well as lofty ideology pervaded with communist revolutionary spirit, can be called a true Communist. This attribute of the Communist is formed and strengthened through a revolutionary organizational life.

Organizational life is a furnace for ideological training and a school for revolutionary education. Only through tightened organizational life can one be steeled and brought up into a real revolutionary loyal to the revolutionary cause of the working class. We should wage a vigorous struggle to strengthen the organizational life of the working people. All people should be brought to take an active part in organizational life, observe organizational discipline of their own accord, faithfully carry out what is entrusted and assigned to them by their organizations, live under the guidance and control of their organizations, and constantly receive revolutionary education.

What is most important in organizational life is to intensify the practice of criticism. To unfold ideological struggle by means of criticism and educate and remold men through ideological struggle—this is the policy consistently followed by our Party in revolutionizing people. All the organizations are required to strengthen the practice of criticism and conduct a strong ideological battle against unsound ideological elements of all descriptions.

To this end, we should resolutely fight, first and foremost, against wrong approaches to criticism and bring people to take a principled attitude toward criticism. Criticism should, in all circumstances, be such as to save comrades and cement unity; it should on no account be criticism for criticism's sake. In making criticism, one must not try to shift the responsibility for one's own faults to others, or to take vengeance for his being criticized, place political stigmas on others at random, or to reprimand the criticized person peremptorily. Also, criticism should be conducted regularly and patiently, not in a shock campaign. We ought to educate all our people in this spirit of principled criticism, thus creating an atmosphere of revolutionary criticism and getting everyone steeled in the midst of criticism. In this way we must see that all people wage an uncompromising fight against negative phenomena in good time and are constantly cultivated, remolded and revolutionized.

An important question posed in carrying out the revolutionizing and "working-classizing" of society is to get rid of the way of life left over from the old society in all domains and establish a new socialist way of life throughout.

The socialist way of life is established in a socialist society; accordingly, to establish the socialist way of life means making all people conduct their activities in the political, economic, cultural and moral realms in accordance with the socialist standards of life and the socialist rules for action.

We have so far scored many successes in the work of establishing a new socialist way of life, but the way of life carried over from the old society still lingers in no small measure in all domains ranging from state activity to private life, which causes obstacles to the building of socialism and to the work of educating and remolding the working people.

We should eliminate the way of life of the old society and

thoroughly establish the socialist way of life in all fields so that all may live and behave in keeping with the intrinsic nature of our society which is based on collectivism. Capitalistic administrative laws and regulations should be done away with in all spheres of state activity, new socialist administrative laws and regulations should be perfected and, especially, socialist order should be fully introduced in economic work. A regular order should be established in socialist economic management and administration so that there may be no room for obsolete ideas in economic management and administration as a whole—from registering and inventorying, keeping and taking care of the property of the country and people, to using and handling common property. It is also necessary to establish a proper order in socialist community life, in the everyday social life of people, and steadily to create the norms of cultural and moral life commensurate with socialist and communist society. Educational work should be intensified to obliterate outdated moral standards extant among the working people and, at the same time, models of a new moral life should be created and popularized one by one through a social movement, the standards of communist morality perfected gradually.

All our Party members and working people, the working class and cooperative farmers and working intellectuals, ought to uphold the Party's line of revolutionizing and "working-classizing," and pursue a vigorous struggle to carry it through. Our Party members and working people must strive to remake themselves on communist lines and revolutionize their families; especially, the leading functionaries, before anybody else, must revolutionize themselves and their families. Beginning with the revolutionizing of families, we should revolutionize sub-work teams, work teams and people's neighborhood units, and then revolutionize work places and *ri*, and gradually revolutionize and "working-classize" the whole of society by means of creating models and generalizing our experiences. We will thus turn all our working people into ardent revolutionaries, true builders of socialism and communism, and firmly unite the whole of society with one ideology, the unitary ideology of our Party, seething with revolutionary spirit and creative zeal, thus hastening the ultimate victory of our revolution.

STRENGTHENING THE NATION'S DEFENSE POWER

The situation in our country is still acute and tense. The aggressive maneuvers of the U.S. imperialists are being further intensified and their plots to provoke another war are becoming more overt. Under the wing of the U.S. imperialists, the Japanese militarists are also stepping up their renewed aggressive maneuvers against Korea. The puppet clique of South Korea, dual stooges of U.S. and Japanese reactionaries, are running about recklessly in an endeavor to execute the war policies of their masters. In our country the danger of war is increasing with every passing day.

To cope with the prevailing situation we must speed up socialist construction to the utmost and strengthen our national defense power at the same time. We should continue to hold fast to the line already put forth by the Party, the line of arming the entire people, turning the whole country into a fortress, converting the whole army into a cadre army and modernizing it, and should implement more thoroughly the principle of self-defense in national defense.

Most important in increasing the defense capabilities of the country is to arm the entire people more adequately. Everyone should learn military affairs in earnest and take a more active part in military training. The workers, peasants and all other working people should always keep themselves fully ready to annihilate the aggressors at any place the enemy attacks, while accelerating socialist construction, with a hammer or sickle in one hand and a rifle in the other. When all the people are under arms, when all the people hate the enemy, when all the people join in fighting against the aggressors, it is quite possible to defeat any enemy.

Our People's Army is entrusted with the honorable mission to safeguard our great socialist gains and the freedom and happiness of the people from the encroachment of the enemy. The People's Army should keep itself fully ready at all times to deal crushing blows at the aggressors in good time and wipe them out, even if the enemy attack us by surprise.

The important task in strengthening the combat power of the People's Army is to fully arm the servicemen politically and ideologically and, on this basis, encourage them always to study and perfect the art of war suited to the actual conditions of our country, and on that groundwork effect the modernization of the army.

Ours is a country with many mountains and rivers and long coastal lines. If we make good use of these topographical conditions to skillfully employ mountain warfare and night actions and properly combine large-unit operations with small-unit operations, regular-army warfare with guerrilla warfare, we are fully able to destroy even an enemy armed to the teeth with the most up-to-date military techniques. This was proved by the experience of the last Fatherland Liberation War in our country and is also proved by the experience of the Vietnam war today.

Therefore, we must base ourselves strictly upon the specific conditions of our country in modernizing the People's Army and developing military science and technique. If we try, instead, mechanically to copy or dogmatically to take over a foreign art of war and foreign weapons and military technical materiel allegedly to modernize the People's Army, it may result in serious harm to our national defense preparations.

We must perfect the art of war in such a way as to make up for the defects in the People's Army, reinforce its weak links and foster its strong points, always in line with the requirements of the Party's military strategic thought based on a full consideration of the concrete conditions of our country and the experience of the last Fatherland Liberation War. On this basis, we must advance our military science and technique and constantly improve the weapons and military technical materiel of the People's Army. We must adhere in all circumstances to the principle of making weapons suitable to the specific conditions of our country and modernizing military equipment commensurate with the level of industrial progress of our country. The combat training of the People's Armymen should also be conducted in such a way as to master the art of war suited to the actual conditions of our country and to fully develop our military science and technique.

Ours is a small and newly-developed country. Frankly speaking, we are not in a position to compete with developed countries in military technical equipment, nor are we required to do so. The destiny of war is by no means decided by modern weapons or military technique. Although the imperialists have a military technical preponderance, our People's Army has on its side politico-ideological superiority over them. The lofty mission and revolutionary spirit of fighting for the freedom and liberation of the fatherland and the people, and the noble traits such as comradeship between officers and men, conscious military discipline and bonds of kinship with the people, are the characteristic features of our People's Army which no imperialist armed forces of aggression can ever possess. Precisely because of such politico-ideological superiority, our People's Army can readily defeat the enemy who is technically preponderant.

In order to reinforce the defense power of the nation, the whole Party and the entire people also should buckle down to a further acceleration of war preparations. All Party members and working people should combat indolence and slackness and always maintain sharp revolutionary vigilance, keeping themselves alert and ready so that they can fight to repulse the enemy without the slightest hesitation no matter when he may attack by surprise. We must never be captivated by a pacifistic mood and, in particular, must strictly guard against the revisionist ideological trend of warphobia to prevent it from infiltrating into our ranks.

The outcome of a war depends largely on whether or not the manpower and material requirements of the front and the rear are fully met over a long duration of time. We should secure an ample reserve of necessary materials by intensifying the struggle for increased production in all fields of the national economy, develop the munitions industry, reorganize the economy in conformity with the demands of the situation, and prepare ourselves in advance to continue production even in case of war. We should, in this way, build up a firm material basis to implement more thoroughly the principle of self-defense in national defense.

Our national defense power is literally of a defensive nature and is designed to defend the security of our country and our people against imperialist aggression. We have no intention to threaten or make aggression against anybody. Threats and aggression against others have nothing to do with the policies of our Party. Our country is a peace-loving socialist country, and our people is a people who loves peace ardently. Due to the inherent nature of our state and social system we consistently advocate peace and are doing all we can to preserve and consolidate peace. No one should, however, take our aspiration and desire for peace and our persevering efforts to preserve it for a sign of weakness. Our people do not want to provoke others first but will never allow anyone to provoke us even a little. We are striving to prevent war, but we are never afraid of it. If the imperialists assault us by force of arms, we shall destroy the aggressors to a man so that they may not return home alive. We shall strengthen the nation's defense power and decisively shatter any surprise attack by the enemy, firmly safeguard the socialist gains and impregnably defend the eastern outpost of socialism.

INDEX

INDEX